Namaste!

Imagine you have a friend in Kathmandu. She has spent years exploring the wonders of Nepal to experience and enjoy the diverse pleasures this ancient land has to offer.

With her experienced recommendations, you could choose to walk breathless in the high mountains, gasp while rafting through the white river waters, and spend a few hours on elephants in search of tiger and rhino in the jungles. She will also guide you through mustard and emerald paddy fields of Kathmandu Valley, lead you to marvel at the grand palaces and dally in the primeval temples.

Your guide is Lisa Choegyal, who has lived in Kathmandu since 1974 and is a Director of the Tiger Mountain Group who pioneer, operate and design adventure and wildlife trips all over Nepal and other remote areas of the subcontinent. She is the producer of the *Insight Guide: Nepal* and *Cityguide: Kathmandu Valley* and contributor to *Insight Guide: South Asia* and *Indian Wildlife.*

Choegyal starts with an overview of the culture and history of Kathmandu Valley, which explains the intricacies of Nepalese life and the culture of its colorful people. She then offers you three full-day itineraries to introduce you to diverse aspects of the famed Valley. This is followed by 14 part and full-day itineraries, using cars or bicycles and on foot, for you to combine as you please. All the musts of Kathmandu Valley are included, as well as some off-the-beaten-track secrets. Five overnight itineraries take you to spectacular places beyond the Valley, such as a drive through the Chinese border and the Himalayan range, so that you can enjoy the mountains, rivers and jungles of this extraordinary country.

Suggestions for dining, shopping and practical information are in the last section. There is a selected glossary to help you interpret the architectural and religious terms that you will encounter daily.

Choegyal wants you to see the Nepal she knows and loves and for you to unravel its mysteries and appreciate its complexities. Hence this book is for the traveler who wants to understand and experience as much as possible in a short time. By all means stray from the set itineraries to perceive this unique, many-layered country – that is what knowing Nepal is all about.

Namaste! Welcome!

Insight Pocket Guide:
Nepal
First Edition

© **1991 APA Publications (HK) Ltd**

All Rights Reserved

Printed in Singapore by
Höfer Press (Pte) Ltd

Nepal

Royal Chitwan National Park

Written by	**Lisa Van Gruisen**
Directed by	**Hans Höfer**
Design Concept by	**V. Barl**
Art Direction by	**Karen Hoisington**
Photography by	**Bill Wassman and others**
Editorial Director	**Michael Stachels**

Contents

What to Know

Maps

It was over fifteen years ago that I first came to Nepal in the course of Asian wanderings. I took myself on a trek in the Annapurnas, became fascinated with Kathmandu Valley, was enticed down to the jungles of Chitwan, and have been here ever since. It was never meant to happen, but time passed and there was always a good reason to remain. Over the years many people have expressed envy at my living in a country which captivates so many with its special magnetism. I continue to feel privileged that it has worked out this way.

That fundamental attraction is still not hard to find, though a little more obscured by the cars, new buildings and dust of modern Kathmandu. These itineraries help you to shake off the spoilt façade of the city and find the enchantment that is waiting to be discovered. My suggestions include a few days spent outside the Valley, where a new world awaits and where little is changed.

It is not just the charm of the people of Nepal, which never ceases to amaze, but the depth of their faith and extent of their traditions that impress visitors. Look, and you will see expressions of this in morning brass trays of offerings or the vermilion *tika* on a forehead. The temples and shrines are used daily as part of life.

You will be entranced at the colors of the Valley, the blue of the sky, the white of the mountains, the greens and yellows of the fields, the earth brown of the village houses and the brilliant colors of the women's clothes. With the clarity of the light and the constant action in the streets, Kathmandu is a photographer's paradise and a traveler's treasure.

You cannot miss the richness of the three great Durbar Squares of Kathmandu, Patan and Bhaktapur and the most famous shrines of Bodhnath, Pashupatinath and Swayambhunath. But go a step beyond to less-trodden corners of the Valley – to the neglected city of Kirtipur, to the temples of Changu Narayan, Vajra Yogini and Chandeshwari (among others), the stupas of Chabahil and Nama Buddha, and distant towns such as Panauti and Pharping. My suggestions may seem to involve a lot of walking, but you will not find it arduous as there is much to delight and distract.

Many of the itineraries overlap and deliberately have you retracing your steps as you will appreciate much more on the relative familiarity of a second visit.

Bicycling around the Valley is a good way to witness life at a manageable speed, but some days you will have to arrange a car. You might prefer a guide to accompany you to help interpret the complexities of the Durbar Squares, for instance, and I recommend all visitors save time and energy by using a travel agent to help smooth the practical details.

The overnight section takes you beyond the Valley, to glimpse in just a few days, the delights of the rivers, jungles and mountains of this amazingly diverse country. Although to many, Kathmandu is considered Nepal, Nepal is certainly not only Kathmandu, as you will discover.

Lisa Choegyal

Lost Horizons

Nepal has long intrigued outsiders with fables of Lost Horizons and Shangri-La. Shrouded in mystery until the 1950s when its borders were first opened to foreigners. Nepal has an astonishing diversity of terrain for such a small country. In one day the organised visitor can fly amidst the world's highest mountains, browse amongst the most beautiful temples and ride elephants in the tall grasslands of the jungles.

A landlocked rectangle that curves along the line of the central Himalaya, Nepal is 553 miles (885 km) long and from 56 to 137 miles (90 to 220 km) wide. The stupendous heights of the white Himalaya, the 'Abode of the Gods', dominate the senses. Eight of the ten highest mountains in the world are within or on Nepal's borders, including the highest, Mount Everest, at 29,028 ft (8,048 m).

Massive rivers plunge through Himalayan gorges as they race from the high Tibetan plateau through the Mahabharat, or middle hills, irrigating the ochre-red terraces, slowing through the fertile farmlands of the Terai and hardwood forests of the Siwalik (Churia) hills

Culture

before eventually draining into the mighty Ganges.

Entirely mountainous except for the narrow strip of the Terai along its southern border, Nepal's climates range from the alpine sub-zero temperatures of the highlands to the tropical heat of the Terai lowlands. Squeezed, physically and politically, between the vastness of China and India, Nepal's 19 million people live in a country roughly the size of England or New Zealand. They are a homogenous mix of cultures and customs and nowhere can this be better appreciated than in Kathmandu Valley.

Valley of Plenty

Situated between the Great Himalayan and the Mahabhara ranges and located almost in the center of Nepal, the broad fertile acres of the Valley of Kathmandu is the obvious choice for its capital. Covering an area of 220 sq miles (570 sq km), the Valley today supports a population of nearly one million people. The alluvial floor is very suitable for growing rice, the staple diet of the Nepalese, and it is well irrigated by the Bagmati River. At an altitude of 4,400 ft (1,350) above sea level, few capital cities enjoy such a clement climate with an unusual amount of sunshine and mean temperatures pleasantly varying between 10° - 36°C (50° - 97°F).

Agriculture plays an important role in the daily life of the inhabitants and the changing cycle of the seasons are marked with the intense greens and yellows of cereal crops, the golden heaps of rice and the vivid reds of chillies. Natural wonders arrest the visitor at every turn in the Kathmandu Valley. Rivers and streams interlace the landscape, the brick red villages cling to ridges to preserve precious land and even from the center of the cities it is possible to catch a glimpse of the snow-capped peaks of the majestic Himalaya against an endless blue sky. Add to this setting the most vibrant element of all: the people of Nepal and their kaleidoscope of culture.

Crossroads of Culture

Nowhere in the world can one find the same concentration of culture, art and tradition that coexist in the Kathmandu Val-

Lowland Terai - following a wedding procession

ley. Isolated by the Himalayan barrier to the north and malarial swamps to the south, Kathmandu Valley is a crucible of culture distilled from centuries of travelers, traders, artists and artisans on their way between the ancient civilisations of China and India. The diversity of the people is immediately visible in the faces of the colorfully-clad crowds who cram the medieval streets of the old cities. The richness of the heritage can be measured in the tangle of temples, shrines, stupas and palaces, one more gloriously decorated and adorned than the next.

Kathmandu is a true cultural crossroads for the more than 30 different ethnic groups who live in the hills and lowland Terai of Nepal, a mosaic that embraces both Aryan and Mongol races, several religions and as many languages and traditions as there are peoples. In addition to the Sanskrit-based official language, Nepali, there are as many as 36 different languages, and many more dialects.

People come to the Kathmandu Valley on holy pilgrimages, to celebrate a special festival or to trade and barter in the bazaars. Many of the hill people still consider the Kathmandu Valley to be 'Nepal'. Thronging the streets you may see people from the north of Tibetan descent, Tamangs, or 'horsemen', and the Sherpas of international mountain climbing fame. From all through the middle hills come Rais, Limbus, Gurungs, Magars and Thakalis and the ubiquitous Brahmans and Chhetris, the high caste warriors. From the Terai lowlands come the aboriginal Tharus and Majhis and many people of Indian origin. The early inhabitants of the Kathmandu Valley, the Newars, are one of the oldest of the ethnic groups, with a language so unusual its origins are still debated.

Sealed for centuries from westerners, a common denominator of the myriad people of Nepal is a national pride and fierce independence, derived perhaps from the fact that Nepal has never been colonised, unlike so many Asian neighbors. Politeness is rated very highly by Nepalis, and to avoid offence remember this and keep any opinions you may have on controversial or political subjects to yourself. You will see portraits everywhere of the King and he is respected and revered as a deity in Nepal.

Every Breath a Prayer

It is easy to believe that there are more gods than people in Kathmandu. The fusion of faith found uniquely in the Valley may be theologically bewildering but it is necessary to understand something of the religions to appreciate its role in the day to day life of the Nepalis people.

It is often hard to distinguish between the two main spiritual currents of Hinduism and Buddhism, especially when they are interwoven with the exotica of Tantrism against a background of animistic cults retained from the distant past. As a very general rule, both Hindu and Buddhist temples may take the pagoda form, the difference is that the *shikara*-style temples are Hindu and the white-dome stupas are Buddhist.

The Hindu pantheon of gods include many colorful characters and fanciful stories. Many of the gods and goddesses appear in different aspects with different names, further confusing the visitor. Hardly a week passes without a festival and daily offerings of flower petals, rice and vermilion powder on a brass tray are proffered in *puja* at the many hundreds of shrines. Ritual sacrifice, whether as a blessing, initiation or as part of a festival, is always a male animal and usually a chicken, goat or buffalo. Sacrifice is a cornerstone of worship in Nepal's Hindu religion.

Many of Kathmandu's Newars are Buddhist, but they will recognise Hindu gods in different forms and likewise, Hindus regard the Buddha as an incarnation of Vishnu. It has been said that if one asks a Newar if he is Hindu or Buddhist, he will reply, "Yes". The question is meaningless and implies an exclusive choice which is foreign to the Newar's religious experience.

Although political leaders have always been Hindu, Buddhism since its emergence in the sixth century, has been tolerated. In the centuries following the life of the Buddha in India, many doctrinal disputes arose, leading to various schisms in the philosophy. Most important was the break between the Theravada school, which today is dominant in Southeast Asia and Sri Lanka, and the Mahayana school, which spread north to Tibet. Tibetan or Mahayana Buddhism became highly developed in the remote vastness of the Tibetan plateau where it absorbed the original shamanisitic *Bon* faith. The followers of the four main sects of Mahayana Buddhism acknowledge the Dalai Lama as

Fine new silk and brocade *thangka*

their spiritual leader. Tibetan Buddhism now thrives in Nepal's atmosphere of religious tolerance. There are many new monasteries at Bodhnath and Swayambhunath, and Lumbini is being restored and developed for visitors.

One cannot speak of religions in Nepal without touching on the practice of Tantrism, a legacy of the pre-Buddhist medieval cultures of India. Tantra is a Sanskrit word, referring to the basic warp of threads in weaving. Literally, Tantrism reiterates the Buddhist philosophy of the essential interweaving of all things and actions. It expanded the realm of Hindu gods, cults and rites and created within Buddhism a major trend which reached great importance in Nepal, often finding expression in esoteric practices.

With such diversity, religious tolerance within Nepal is of the essence. Over the centuries all the masterpieces of art produced by the great civilisations of the Kathmandu Valley are almost entirely religious in character; whether architecture, sculpture, woodcarving, metalwork, literature, music or dance, the marvellous legacy left by the early Newar artists and craftsmen is all inspired by their gods. No visitor can fail to be impressed by the wealth of richness to be found literally lying around, the heritage of previous generations. The creative and turbulent history of the country explains many apparent conundrums.

The Legend of the Lake

In the distant dawn of unrecorded time when deities mingled with mortals, the Valley of Kathmandu was a turquoise lake on which floated a white lotus flower from which emanated an awesome flame. Wishing to worship the flame more closely, the Buddhist patriarch Manjushri came from his mountain retreat in China and sliced the restraining Valley wall with his sacred sword so that the lotus might settle on what is now the hill of Swayambhunath.

A Hindu version of the story is that Krishna released the waters by hurling a thunderbolt at the Valley wall. Whatever the fiction, the fact is, geologists confirm the Kathmandu Valley was once under water and the Chobar gorge is not only as narrow as a blade but below it, enshrined in a temple, is a stone that some believe is Krishna's thunderbolt.

The evocative mythology of early Nepal gradually dissolves as, after several successive waves of hazy Tibeto-Burman migrants, the dynasty of Kirati kings gradually comes into historic focus in the seventh or eighth century B.C. These apparently fierce tribal people invaded from the east and may have been the Kiriaths of Old Testament Babylon. Buddha was born as Prince Siddharta Gautama in Lumbini in south Nepal during the reign of the 28 Kirati kings — the actual date of 543 B.C. is disputed. Two centuries later the great Indian emperor Ashoka embraced Buddhism and converted his empire. He visited Lumbini, raised the engraved column and is believed to have visited the Kathmandu Valley and had the Ashoka stupas

Pokhara - boats on Phewa Lake

built in Patan, though there is no actual proof.

Licchavi Legacy

When the Kiratis had succumbed to the Licchavi invasion from India in about A.D. 300, the first golden age of Nepalese art flourished and stone sculptures survive today as a testament to the skill of their craftsmen. The oldest inscription in the Valley, A.D. 467, is on a stone pillar at Changu Narayan, confirming King Manadeva I as a king of considerable talents, responsible for expanding his empire both to the east and west. The Licchavis also laid down the hierarchical structure of society, according to the Hindu caste system.

The three Thakuri dynasties began in A.D. 602 with the ascent of King Amsuvarman, who married his sister to an Indian prince and his daughter, Bhrikuti, to Tibet's powerful King Tsrong-tsong Gompo. Bhrikuti is believed to have taken, as part of her dowry, the begging bowl of the Buddha. Her role in converting Tibet to Buddhism has made her a legendary figure, reincarnated as the Green Tara. The Thakuris inaugurated the three great festivals of Indrajatra, Krishna Jayanti and the Machhendranath Jatras and it was during their time that the Kasthamandap or "Pavilion of Wood" was constructed from a single tree, giving Kathmandu its name. This period lasted until 1200 and is termed Nepal's "Dark Ages" as so little else is known of this period of obscure turmoil.

Marvellous Mallas

The Malla kings controlled Nepal from the 13th to 18th centuries during a predominantly stable age of peace and plenty. It was the Malla kings who established the custom of being considered incarnations of Vishnu, as are the present Shah rulers. They adopted the Taleju Bhawani from South India as the royal goddess of Nepal. Although they were strict Hindus, they were tolerant of Buddhism which was widespread among the people, especially in its Tantric form. They developed the familiar compact villages seen today in the Valley using brick and tiles for the first time and clustered together to preserve limited arable land and as protection against bandits.

The Mallas survived a stormy period of

Bhaktapur - King Bhupathindra Malla gold statue

earthquakes and the brief Moslem invasion of 1336. By the early 15th century they had introduced Newari as the court language and chosen Bhaktapur as their capital. A renaissance of art and culture flourished, the foundation of what we see today. The dividing of the Valley in 1482 into three separate kingdoms, those of Kathmandu, Patan (Lalitpur) and Bhaktapur (Bhadgaon), no doubt encouraged each to compete with the next to glorify their palaces and temples, but led eventually to the downfall of their dynasty.

Shah Supremacy

Political rivalries amongst the divided city-states led to their demise. The opportunity was seized by the King of Gorkha, then a principality situated halfway between Kirtipur and Pokhara, and which had been growing in strength under the dynamic leadership of King Prithvi Narayan Shah. After 10 years of preparation from his fort at Nuwakot, the founder of modern Nepal took Kathmandu and Patan by force in 1768 and Bhaktapur and Kathmandu yielded to him in 1769 by trickery and intrigue. The Valley was unified and he established Kathmandu as his capital. King Prithvi Narayan Shah and his descendants, consolidated and expanded the new empire until it stretched from Kashmir to Sikkim, double its present size.

This led to inevitable conflicts with neighbors and the Chinese were eventually called in by the Tibetans to curb Nepal's expansionist ambitions to the north. An agreement was reached in 1792 which forced Nepal to desist.

A full-scale war with British India lasted from 1814 to 1816 and ended in the Treaty of Friendship signed at Segauli which shrank the borders to their present size and established a permanent British presence in Kathmandu. Brian Hodgeson was not the first Westerner to visit the fabled Valley. The first British envoy, William Kirkpatrick, had visited in 1792 with regard to the disputes with Tibet, and the Italian Capuchins had been permitted a mission as early as 1730.

There is an interesting footnote to this period. The gallantry the Gorkha soldiers displayed in the 1816 conflict so impressed the British that they enlisted them into the British Indian Army. Even today, the Gurkhas, as they are now called, are recognised as outstanding soldiers by the British and Indians.

Rana Rule

In 1846, taking advantage of palace intrigues, the "Kot Massacre" was staged by the shrewd and enterprising Jung Bahadur Rana, who designated himself as prime minister, and later "maharajah", with powers superior to those of the sovereign. He made his office hereditary, establishing a unique line of succession that went first to brothers and only then to sons. Ruthlessly suppressing all opposition, he took the highly unusual step of travelling to Europe and was much impressed with Queen Victoria and the fashions of the day. On his return, he launched a frivolous vogue of neo-classical palaces, and ladies of the court arranged their *saris* to look like crinolines.

In all other respects, however, travel remained limited to a privileged few and foreigners were treated with extreme distrust. Although some reforms and advances took place during the century of Rana rule, they are generally criticised for running Nepal as their own private feudal estate and not doing enough for the country.

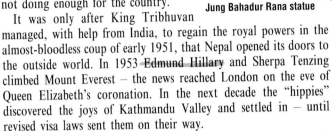

Jung Bahadur Rana statue

It was only after King Tribhuvan managed, with help from India, to regain the royal powers in the almost-bloodless coup of early 1951, that Nepal opened its doors to the outside world. In 1953 Edmund Hillary and Sherpa Tenzing climbed Mount Everest – the news reached London on the eve of Queen Elizabeth's coronation. In the next decade the "hippies" discovered the joys of Kathmandu Valley and settled in – until revised visa laws sent them on their way.

Despite early intentions, it was not until 1959 that Tribhuvan's son, King Mahendra, established a constitution that provided for a parliamentary system of government. The first general election in Nepal's history took place over several months in that year but the experiment with democracy was short-lived and ended in 1960 with the King taking back power. The 1962 constitution established the *panchayat* system, an administrative and legislative system culminating in an indirectly-elected national legislature, with the prime minister and cabinet appointed by the King.

King Mahendra died in 1972, and was succeeded by his son, the youthful King Birendra, who declared as his goal the improvement of the standard of living of his people. A referendum in 1980 reconfirmed the people's support of the monarchy, but by April 1990 popular dissatisfaction with the lack of reforms and corrupt officials erupted into demonstrations and riots in Kathmandu. The ban on the multi-party system was lifted and an interim government appointed to prepare a democratic constitution and arrange a general election.

Nepal Now

King Birendra Bir Bikram Shah Dev today heads the only Hindu kingdom in the world. He is faced with some Himalayan sized problems, bringing his country into the 21st century to reach his goal of providing basic needs to the people by the year 2000. The population is increasing at the annual rate of 2.6 percent and rural poverty remains the chief problem. Foreign aid is a large component in Nepal's development budget and the nation's precarious position as a Himalayan buffer state between India and China may still be its best guarantee of survival, a foreign policy unchanged for centuries.

HISTORY

8th century B.C.-A.D. 300: The history of the eastern Kiriath kings are inextricably interwoven with legend.

A.D. 300-700: The first golden age of Nepalese arts flourish in the Licchavi dynasty. The Valley's earliest stone inscription describes Nepal's first great historical figure, King Manadeva I. Leaving a legacy of superb stone sculptures, the Licchavis instigate the tradition of a hierarchical Hindu caste society.

A.D. 602-1200: The "Dark Ages" of turmoil under the Thakuris, probably from northern India. Princess Bhrikuti of Nepal marries King Tsrong-tsong Gompo of Tibet and is deified as the Green Tara for converting him and Tibet to Buddhism, along with her Chinese co-wife, the White Tara.

1200: King Ari-deva assumes the title Malla, and founds a new, highly-accomplished dynasty. Probably noble fugitives of the Muslim invasion of Rajasthan, the Mallas bring riches and recognition to Nepal, reinforce the caste system and establish the villages familiar to us today.

1336: The Mallas survive a raid by the Sultan of Bengal. By the 15th century a renaissance flourishes and many great buildings, fine woodcarving and powerful sculpture seen today belong to this period.

1482: King Yaksha Malla dies; the Valley is divided and ruled as three city-states: Kathmandu, Patan (Lalitpur) and Bhaktapur (Bhadgaon). Agriculture and cottage industries thrive but political rivalries fragment the empire.

1768: Prithvi Narayan Shah, ruler of Gorkha, conquers Kathmandu and Patan and takes Bhaktapur a year later, thus founding a united Nepal and the present Shah dynasty. Expansionist policies and conflicts of trading interests lead to clashes with Nepal's neighbors.

1792: Invasion by Chinese troops follows several wars with Tibet. Nepal has to pledge to desist from attacking Tibet and to pay tribute regularly to the Chinese emperor in Peking.

1816: "Treaty of Friendship" signed; ends two years of war with British India. Nepal's territory is cut in half to its present borders. A British representative is established in Kathmandu, the first and only Western envoy resident in Nepal.

1846: Jung Bahadur Rana takes advantage of palace intrigue to stage the "Kot Massacre" and establishes the Rana regime of hereditary ruling prime ministers. The Ranas rule Nepal, virtually keeping the royal family prisoners for ceremonial and religious purposes.

1951: King Tribhuvan regains royal power, aided by recently independent India. Foreigners are now allowed into Nepal and two years later, Mount Everest is climbed.

1962: After an unsuccessful experiment with parliamentary rule, King Mahendra institutes the basic system of *panchayat* government.

1972: King Birendra succeeds to the throne on the death of his father, King Mahendra.

1980: A national referendum is called by King Birendra following unrest, and reaffirms the people's confidence in the *panchayat* system. The constitution is further amended to give the electorate more powers.

1990 : Following violent demonstrations and riots, King Birendra announces on 8 April that the legal ban on political parties is lifted and appoints an interim government to prepare a democratic constitution for Nepal.

ne King and Queen during oronation ceremonies

Day Itinerarie

Everyone who arrives in Kathmandu is exhilarated, either by the clear sparkling views, the friendly smiling people or the excitement of arriving (or returning) to a city they have long dreamed of. These first three days are designed to crystalise that exhiliration.

After only three days you will have experienced palaces and bazaars, temples and tigers, culture and countryside. Make sure your shoes are made for walking.

If you arrive in the morning after spending time in India, you might want to go that first afternoon to Patan (Pick and Choose 1).

DAY 1

Gentle Introduction

Wander in the medieval magic of the Kathmandu Durbar Square, visiting the Temple of the Living Goddess, Kasthamandap and the Hanuman Dhoka Durbar. Walk through the colorful bazaars of Asan and Indrachowk. Lunch in the peaceful garden at Mike's

Breakfast. **Grab a cab round the Ring Road to Chabahil and linger at the stupa of Bodhnath, one of the great sights of the Valley. Drive through the countryside to the Gokarna Mahadev temple.**

Although Nepalis live with the light, the morning mist in the winter makes it pointless leaving your hotel until 9.30 a.m., after a leisurely breakfast. Spring and early autumn are more inspiring for an early start.

From the **Tundhikhel**, the central parade ground that separates the new city from the old, walk under the arch and up **New Road**, so-called as it was rebuilt after the terrible earthquake of 1934. It is lined with shops selling imported goods, drugs and jewels but they do not open early.

At the top you enter a different world. On your left is forgotten **Freak Street**, the abandoned hangout of the 1960s hippies and flower children, and nearby is the raised brick platform of **Basantapur,** formerly the home of royal elephants.

Kathmandu Durbar Square

(a) Kumari Bahal
(b) Temple of Narayan
(c) Kasthamandap
(d) Ashok Binayak
(e) Shiva Temple
(f) Shiva-Parvati Temple House
(g) King Pratap Malla
(h) Degu Taleju Temple
(i) Basantapur Tower
(j) Hanuman Dhoka
(k) Nasal Chowk
(l) Mohan Chowk
(m) Sundari Chowk
(n) Basanpur Tower
(o) Kirtipur Tower
(p) Lalitpur Tower
(q) Bhaktapur Tower
(r) Lohan Chowk
(s) Pancha Mukhi Hanuman
(t) Jagnnath Temple
(u) Gopoinath Mandir
(v) Taleju Temple
(w) Tarana Devi Mandir

Ahead is the **Kathmandu Durbar Square**, the hub of the old city at the crossroads of diagonal trade routes. Founded by the Licchavi kings in the 8th century, this profusion of over 50 temples and

Gairi Dhara

Tangal

Police HQ

Maneswari

Harigaon

Sita
Bhawan

vancaur

andir

Bhagwati

Sanu
Gaucharan

Gyaneswar

Gyaneswar

Maitidevi

Maiti Devi

ar

Kalikasthan

Baneswar

Singha Durbar

Dhobi Khola

Baneswar

Mahal

⑤

Baneswar

Chabahil

to Bodhnatz

Candrabinayak

Chabahil Stupa

Siphal

Deopatan

Bhandarkhal

Jayabageswari

Pashupatinath

Bhuwaneswari

Banakali

Ring Road

Battisputali

Marg

Dewkota

Bagmati

Dhobi Khola

Hotels:
1 Ambassador
2 Annapurna
3 Blue Star
4 Crystal
5 Everest International
6 Kathmandu Guesthouse
7 Malla
8 Manang
9 Mayalu
10 Mt. Makalu
11 Nook
12 Panorama
13 Siddharta
14 Star
15 Woodlands

Kathmandu City - Day 1
400 m/ 0,25 miles

Hanuman Dhoka Palace – wood-carved window

monuments is a living museum to the glorious Malla dynasty architecture, with some additions by King Prithvi Narayan Shah and the Ranas.

You first encounter the **Kumari Bahal** on the left, the mid 18th-century temple of the **Kumari** or Living Goddess. The inner façades, like the main one, have beautifully carved windows and it is here that she can sometimes be persuaded to appear to her admirers. A virgin chosen from the Sakya clan of goldsmiths, the **Kumari** never leaves the sanctuary of her temple except when she is ceremoniously paraded in her chariot at the festival of Indrajatra, when even the King pays her homage.

Ahead, the **Kasthamandap** is at the entrance of the **Maru Tole**, the original Pavilion of Wood said to have been constructed from a single sacred tree, and from where Kathmandu gets its name. Originally a community center it is now a temple dedicated to Gorakhnath. Pause at the golden **Maru Ganesh** shrine, a monument of great importance and always very busy with devotees ensuring their safety before leaving on a journey.

Rest on the nine steps of the **Shiva Temple** whilst admiring the crudely carved deities surveying the scene from the window of the **Shiva-Parvati Temple House**. As you leave the main square, note the great drums on your left which are beaten during the worship of the **Degu Taleju** in her temple opposite. The north-facing door is panelled in silver and the 92-ft (28-m) high roof is capped with a very fine pinnacle. The proud statue of **King Pratap Malla**, who is responsible for much of this glory, is set high on a pillar opposite. Before you move on, notice the large golden mask of **Bhairav** erected in 1796, normally kept screened from public view except during the festival of Indrajatra when *chang* or local beer pours from his mouth and down the throats of the excited crowd.

Now you are in a second square, that is dominated by the

towering **Taleju Bhawani Temple**, the royal deity, whose inner sanctum can only be entered by the King. Built in 1564 by Mahendra Malla, this used to be the highest structure in Kathmandu and at 121 ft (37 m) it was considered inauspicious to build higher.

The entrance to the sprawling old Royal Palace, the **Hanuman Dhoka Durbar**, is a brightly painted gate (open 10 a.m. to 4 p.m., closed every Tuesday), flanked by stone lions and guarded by the palace's namesake, Hanuman, the monkey god, a red-smeared image which dates from 1672. Pass through the golden doors and there is much to explore in this series of superb courtyards, beautifully decorated and still used by the Royal family for ceremonies.

Admire incomparable woodcarving, the King Tribhuvan museum in the **Nasal Chowk** and orient yourself from the nine-storey **Basan-**

Taleju Bhawani Temple

tapur **Tower**. The **Kirtipur Tower** has a domed copper roof, the **Bhaktapur Tower** is of an octagonal form and the **Lalitpur Tower** overlooks New Road. The towers were named after the towns that donated and built them in recognition of the unification of Nepal by King Prithvi Narayan Shah.

The Hanuman Dhoka Durbar was extensively and carefully restored by UNESCO for King Birendra's coronation in February, 1975, which had been delayed until the most auspicious day.

Leave behind the marvels of art and architecture, return to the square and turn right past the fearsome features of the much revered **Black Bhairav**, and shudder at the bloodshed in the **Kot**, the armory where Jung Bahadur enacted his merciless coup in 1846 by murdering most of those in power. The half-buried **Garuda** at the entrance to **Makhan Tole** is evocative of former times and street levels.

Leaving the Durbar Square, the road narrows through the bazaar heading in a northeasterly direction. There are many shrines, courtyards and shops to investigate as you jostle with colorfully-costumed people and honking rickshaws.

At **Indrachowk**, detour into the **Bead Market** through the smallest of passages behind the house opposite the many-balconied **Akash Bhairav**. Sitting in their adjacent booths, the shopkeepers will twist together a bewildering array of multicoloured glass beads to your specifications.

At the next junction, **Kel Tole**, step left through a small gate which leads you into the important **Seto Machhendranath Temple,** home of the guardian deity of Kathmandu, before continuing to the throng of **Asan Tole.** Your senses are bombarded with sights, sounds and smells. Keep walking straight ahead and you emerge from the bazaar at a square pond, the **Rani Pokhari**, with a domed Shiva shrine in the middle, built in 1670 by King Pratap Malla to console his queen

Indrachᴏ

on the death of their son.

Cross the road, but not before noting where you can rent a bicycle, and head along **Jamal Tole** to **Durbar Marg**, the wide avenue where most of the travel agents and airlines are to be found. The **Narayanhitty Royal Palace** is in front of you, named after the water spout which is at the top on the right.

Half-way up Durbar Marg, turn right under the Yak and Yeti Hotel arch. **Mike's Breakfast**, to whose peaceful garden you are heading for lunch, is down the lane first to your right. Order a fresh lime soda while you check the menu for the daily special or select from the generous quiches and iodine-cleansed salads.

When you feel refreshed, take a taxi or better still, arrange a hired car and head north past the Royal Palace up **Lazimpat** and **Maharajgunj**, the area where many foreign missions are found, past the two Princes' palaces to the **Ring Road**, which circles the city. This is not the most direct route to **Bodhnath** but it gives you a chance to gauge the size of the city and appreciate its rural nature. On a clear day the white peaks of **Ganesh Himal** and **Dorje Lakpa** can be seen all across the rice fields and distant foothills.

Bodnath Stupa

It is worth stopping at the stupa of **Chabahil**, one of the very earliest settlements in the Valley, now rather dilapidated. Chabahil stupa is said to have been constructed from materials left over from Bodhnath. There are some early images, interesting *chaityas* and the remains of a *bahal* behind the stupa supposedly founded by Charumati, the daughter of King Asoka.

To the west about 650 ft (200 m) is the beautiful Ganesh shrine of **Chandra Binayak** which is believed to cure diseases and injuries. A brass shrew waits for Ganesh, the helpful son of Shiva, atop a pillar in front of the shrine, resplendent under a modern light.

Spend time lingering at **Bodhnath**, the largest stupa in the Valley whose great dome rises out of the paddy fields against a brilliant blue sky, with a backdrop of white Himalayan peaks. Shaped like a massive *mandala*, which is best discerned from the air, and decorated with strings of fluttering prayer flags, Bodhnath has always been a centre for trade with Tibet and has long links with Lhasa. The all-seeing eyes on the stupa follow Buddhist pilgrims from Tibet, Ladakh, Bhutan and the northern parts of Nepal as they circumambulate clockwise, spinning the embossed prayer wheels. Along the base of the great hemispherical stupa are a ring of 108 small inset images of the Buddha.

To get a glimpse of Buddhist life, explore the surrounding monasteries, many of which are newly built by Western as well as local donors. Bodhnath has become one of the most important Tibetan Buddhist centers in the world.

A charming legend obscures the ancient origins of Bodhnath. It is said that a girl called Kangma built the stupa. Having been banished from heaven by Indra for stealing flowers, she was reborn, as punishment, the daughter of a swineherd.

On earth she had four children, was widowed then managed to make a fortune as a goose girl. She asked the king to give her as much land as the hide of a buffalo would cover, so that she could build a noble temple to the Buddha. The king agreed and the clever girl cut the hide into thin strips, joined them and stretched them out to encircle the land on which Bodhnath now stands.

Do not miss the shopping opportunities at the stalls and small shops that surround the stupa – trinkets mixed among carpets and ethnic fabrics. Look out for the special little shop selling jackets and waistcoats, made from the wool cloth normally used by monks and trimmed with antique ribbon.

Drive on and when the forest of Gokarna comes into sight, turn left and follow the road that winds through the fields on its way to **Sundarijal**, one of the Valley's main water supply. After about three miles (five km) you reach the little village of Gokarna.

The **Gokarna Mahadev** is on the right of the road, a beautifully restored triple-roofed shrine on the banks of the sacred Bagmati with superb carved roof struts. At the **Gokarna Aunshi** festival in June or July, devotees whose fathers have died in the past year must come here and ritually bathe in the river. A particularly fine image of Parvati, Shiva's consort, is enshrined at the northwest corner, though she has recently been modestly garbed to shield her beauty.

After relaxing at your hotel, dine Nepali at the **Bhancha Ghar** restaurant (Tel: 225-172) in Kamaladi, where there is handicraft demonstration, or at the Soaltee Oberoi's **Himalchuli** restaurant (Tel: 272-550) where you can enjoy an 8 p.m. cultural show, staged every evening.

DAY 2

Palaces and Temples

Drive to the ancient city of Bhaktapur, then walk through the Durbar Square, the Tamaudi Square with the five-roofed Nyatapola Temple and the Dattatreya Square before driving on outside the Valley to the Dhulikhel Mountain Resort for lunch with a view.

Return to Banepa and the Chandeshwari temple, with its extraordinary fresco of Bhairav. Visit the classic Newar town of Panauti with its important temples.

Bhairab Nath Stupa

Arrange a car for the day and drive to **Bhaktapur**, also known by its old name of Bhadgoan. Leave it at the entrance to the **Durbar Square**. This most charming of the three Durbar Squares has the best preserved, 'medieval' character and immediately evident is the relative sparseness due to the destruction by the 1934 earthquake.

Opposite the gilded copper **Sun Dhoka (Golden Gate)**, erected in 1753 and hailed as one of the greatest single pieces of Nepali art, is the lovely statue of **Bupathindra Malla** on his tall pillar of stone. Passing through the gate, walk left into the **Mul Chowk** and explore as far as you can before being stopped by guards from entering the sacred and richly ornamented **Taleju Chowk** and **Kumari Chowk**. You are permitted to see the sunken bathing pool known as the **Nag Pokhari**, with its beautiful gilded water spout.

Returning to the main square, notice the octagonal pavilion, the **Chaysiln Mandap**, which has taken three painstaking years to reconstruct from contemporary drawings, on its original plinth. Donated

Harasiddhi Temple detail

to the people of Nepal by Chancellor Kohl of West Germany, the exquisite woodcarving is a tribute to today's craftsmen and the shameless steel girders a tribute to German technology.

Adjacent to the Sun Dhoka is the **Royal Palace of 55 Windows**, rebuilt after it was almost completely destroyed by the 1934 earthquake. Examine the *thangkas* in the recently rearranged **National Art Gallery**, which is in another part of the palace located through a gateway flanked by Hanuman and Narsingh, the man-lion. Before you leave, note the **Sundari Chowk**, the ritual bathing courtyard of the Bhaktapur kings, no longer surrounded by any buildings.

Leave by the **Tamaudi Tole**, a narrow street leading down to the **Tamaudi Square**, lined with tempting shops selling *thangkas*, puppets and artefacts. On your left is the superb five-roofed **Nyatapola Temple** on its five plinths, one of the tallest in the Valley at over 98 ft (30 m) high, dedicated to a mysterious tantric goddess. Notice the pairs of guardians who flank the main staircase, each ten times stronger than the one below. Thus the Malla wrestlers on the bottom plinth are ten times as strong as ordinary men but only one tenth as powerful as the elephants above them, and so on. It is told that King Bupathindra Malla himself carried bricks for the building of the temple to inspire the locals.

At right angles is the earlier **Kasi Bishwanath Temple**, whose Bhairav is paraded at the frenetic annual *Bisket* festival at the Nepali New Year. Pause for a cup of Nepali

Bhaktapur Durbar Square
(a) gateway
(b) Rameshar Temple dedicated to Shiva
(c) Temple dedicated to Durga
(d) Bupathindra Malla
(e) Sun Dhoka
(f) Royal Palace
(g) National Art Gallery
(h) Taleju Chowk
(i) Kumari Chowk
(j) Sundari Chowk
(k) Dharmasala
(l) Tadhunchen Bahal
(m) Batsala Durga
(n) Pashputi Temple

chiya (tea brewed together with milk, sugar and spices) in the temple cafe and enjoy the busy life of the Square. The black saris edged in red are unique to the Newar women of Bhaktapur. Notice the *jyapus*, the Newari farmers, carrying their loads in two baskets strung on a pole across their shoulders. Only Newars use this method of carrying, all the other people of Nepal prefer to use the *dhoko*, or basket, supported on their backs by a strap around their foreheads.

Detour south from here, if you wish, to the **Pottery Market,** then return and walk on down the brick paved streets, via the **Golmadi Tole**, past the little **Golmadi Ganesh Shrine** to the eastern part of Bhaktapur and the **Dattatreya Square**.

Dhulikhel Mountain Resort

The **Dattatreya Temple** is the oldest in this area, as can be devised from its squat shape, not dissimilar to the Kasthamandap in Kathmandu. Considered to be one of the most important temples in the Valley, and serving as both a place of rest and a shrine, the front part (added later) houses the images of Dattatreya, honored as Shiva's teacher.

Down a side alley behind it is the famed (though somewhat overrated) **Peacock Window**. Do not miss the **Woodcarving Museum** nearby in the ancient priest's house, the **Pujari Math**, and formerly the headquarters of the German Bhaktapur Development Project which restored much of the city. Have the car meet you behind the **Nava Durga,** a rather sinister and highly revered temple that is the focus of the ritual masked dancing during festivals.

It is a very pleasant 45-minute drive through the countryside to the **Dhulikhel Mountain Resort** (Tel: 011-61088) for lunch on the road to Tibet. As you leave the Valley at the village of **Sanga**, pause to look back at the panoramic view. The Resort is several miles on past the town of Dhulikhel and do not be tempted to stop at any of the other hostelries. At the Dhulikhel Mountain Resort, perched high above the road, ask to eat outside in the garden to enjoy the mountain views. The marinated chicken kebab is excellent. If you are filled with energy, walk along the ridge for an hour or so above the resort to the little shrine beneath a big tree.

From Dhulikhel drive back down the road to Kathmandu and turn right (north) at the statue of King Tribhuvan in the middle of **Banepa**, a thriving town with many new buildings. Follow the road right and, if you have a genuine interest, call in at the **Banepa Adventist Hospital**. Any old clothes, medicines and donations are made excellent use of in this busy general hospital which serves an impressively large area.

Drive a little further, as far as you can, until the golden roof of the **Chandeshwari Temple** comes into view on the edge of a steep

Mahadev Temple

gorge. The forest above was believed to have been once full of demon beasts and the goddess Parvati was called upon to slay their leader, Chand. The shrine was built in her honor and in the sanctum, there is a fine image of Chandeshwari, the Master of the Slayer of Chand. The multi-colored fresco of Bhairav is worth the trip.

Returning to the Banepa crossroads, the classic Newar town of **Panauti** is a 20-minute drive straight across, a settlement which is possibly pre-Licchavi in origin and a thriving trading town in Malla times. Leave the car at the confluence of the **Pungamati River** and visit the exquisite **Brahmayani Temple**, restored a few years ago by French experts. Cross by the suspension foot bridge and explore the scenic melange of ancient temples and *ghats*. There is a Krishna temple and several Shiva *lingums*.

Walk right to the magnificent **Indreshwar Mahadev**, one of the oldest existing temple structures with some of the earliest woodcarving to be found in Nepal. Founded as early as the 12th and 13th century, the carved wood roof struts are masterly in their elegant simplicity, though earthquake damage from 1988 is threatening their survival. Inside its walled courtyard, note the **Narayan Temple** opposite. Panauti is the end of your walk in Itinerary 14.

From Panauti it is less than an hour back to Kathmandu. Indian kebabs, *tikas*, curries and sitar music at the **Ghar e Kebab** (Tel: 221-711) on Durbar Marg may appeal this evening or perhaps Tibetan food at the **Sunkosi** (Tel: 220-299) in Durbar Marg. Try the *thukpa*, a thick noodle soup, and fried *momos*, a delicious kind of *ravioli* popular with Tibetans.

A Walk in the Country

An early start by car via Sano Thimi to Nagarkot, high on the rim of the Valley. Walk for about three hours part way down the hill along a ridge with views across the Valley, picnicking en route, to the wonderful temple of Changu Narayan. Ancient sculptures litter the courtyard and here is the earliest inscription in the Valley. An evening stroll in Chetrapati and Thamel with a European dinner at Coppers Restaurant.

After an early breakfast, this morning you should leave by 8.30 a.m. with an arranged car for Nagarkot (6,886 ft /2,099 m). Take something warm to wear, a packed lunch and a water bottle. Enjoy the old back road via **Sano Thimi**, where the terracotta animals are sold by the roadside. Look out for the particularly engaging painted figures of the King and Queen. Turn off left behind Bhaktapur, past the "industrial estate" which produces glazed pottery and handmade paper for UNICEF cards, available in the craft shops opposite the Himalaya Hotel in Patan.

The road to **Nagarkot** winds upward through fields, then pine trees, and you can feel the temperature dropping as you climb. Identify the ridge along which you will be walking later by picking

out the gold roofs of Changu Narayan on the left. The view of the receding tiers of blue-grey hills culminating in the white snows well rewards the one-hour drive. Have coffee at one of the friendly small hotels up here. If the weather is really overcast, do not bother going all the way to the top.

Leave the car half way down the hill at the saddle where the ridge joins the road, making sure the driver is clear as to where to meet you – by the teashop on the Sankhu Road below Changu.

The first 20 minutes up through a pine plantation to the crest is the only uphill climb of the day! The walk is a leisurely, three-hour stroll along the ridge line with stunning views across the Valley to the high mountains. If you need reassurance, there is always someone to ask the way. Note the traces of an old Rana irrigation system and the orange pumpkins and red chillies drying on the roofs. The glittering pinnacles of Changu Narayan tempt you on through charming Chhetri and Gurung villages and past curious children. It is more peaceful to eat your picnic by the trail before you reach the village of Changu.

At the top of the main street is the superb temple complex of **Changu Narayan**, rebuilt in 1702 but with the Valley's earliest inscription on a pillar dating its origins to A.D. 464. Marvel at the treasury of priceless Licchavi sculptures of Vishnu and Garuda images, the statues of Bupathindra Malla in a gilded cage and the unusual brickwork on the platform. Changu Narayan is designated a World Heritage Site by UNESCO, one of seven sites in the Kathmandu Valley, which has the distinction of having the largest concentration of World Heritage Sites to be found in the world.

Leave by the west door of this extraordinary and important place, descend down a well-worn path and head for the Manohara River through which you may have to wade unless you find a makeshift bridge. Negotiate the paddy fields to where your car will be waiting beside a cluster of houses and a little tea shop.

After freshening up at your hotel, enjoy an early evening wander in the fading light, starting at the Crystal Hotel at the top of New Road and walking as straight as you can through the maze of the now familiar bazaar area. Look up to catch faces at carved windows and the lilt of an evening song.

Detour right to the **Mahabodha Stupa** and the evening surgery of the famous ayurvedic Doctor Mana Bajracharya – ask anyone where to find his courtyard. Pass some crumbling classic *bahals*, or courtyards, and soon you reach the up-beat, world-traveler area of **Chetrapati** and **Thamel** with lodges, trekking shops and loud music. Note where to rent a bicycle for future reference. Stop for a Star beer or a Khukri rum and coke – and some people-watching – at **Rumdoodle** across from the Kathmandu Guest House, or at **Spam's Spot** further on, the closest bar to an English pub in Kathmandu.

By 7 or 7.30 p.m. you will be ready to emerge into **Keshar Mahal**. Climb the unpromising stairs to the stylish oasis of **Coppers Restaurant** (Tel: 417-095), a favorite with local residents, specialising in delicious English and European dishes. Try the homemade *pate*, charcoal-grill specialities and fresh fruit daiquiris.

Returning to your hotel, notice the **Keshar Library** on the corner, now the **Ministry of Education**, housing a collection of books and old hunting photographs in a musty Rana palace atmosphere. This is a wonderful place to while away a few fascinating hours (open 10 a.m. to 4 p.m., closed Saturdays).

Pick & Choose

These half days are deliberately designed to allow time to wander, look and absorb. If you find them too leisurely, keep moving and combine three in one day. Except where specified, these suggestions are suitable for both mornings and afternoons. The Valley is easy and safe to get around in and you are encouraged to improvise and deviate from the itineraries.

1. Palaces of Patan

Explore the Durbar Square then walk to the Golden Temple, Kumbeshwar Temple and Maha Baudha.

Cycle or taxi to **Patan**, cradle of traditional arts and architecture in the Valley, which is also known by its ancient name of Lalitpur, the Beautiful City. The **Patan Durbar Square** is in the very heart of the city and must rank as one of the very finest urban streetscapes in the world. Visit the courtyards of the **Royal Palace**, more accessible than their Kathmandu counterparts.

Gilded metalwork is a feature of Patan

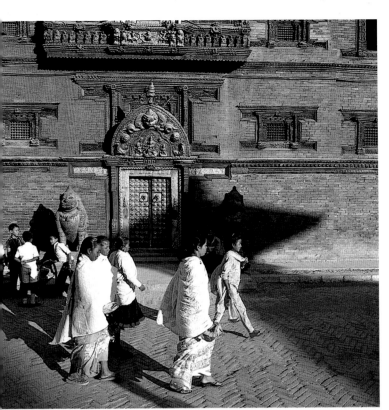
Sundar Chowk Temple – golden door

The present palace structure was built in the 17th century on earlier foundations. The first courtyard, the **Sundari Chowk**, the royal living quarters, was finished in 1627. It contains the spectacular **Tusa Hiti**, the royal bathing tank with a water spout in the form of a gilded conch shell. Lined with hundreds of deities of stone and metal and in an octagonal form to emphasise the king's devotion to the eight *nagas* or serpents, the perimeter of the sunken tank is guarded by a pair of dragons carved in stone.

The entrance to the Sundari Chowk is through a very narrow doorway, to the left of a more impressive entrance which is never used as it is believed to be controlled by an evil spirit. The next courtyard, the **Mul Chowk,** was completed in 1666, and has the gilded sanctuary of the **Bidya Mandir** shrine in its center. Another favourite house goddess of the Malla kings is enshrined in the south wing of the courtyard, guarded by life-size gilded bronze figures. The **Taleju Temple** is in the north eastern corner, and can only be entered by her priests. Note the fine doorway, a tribute to the metalworking castes for which Patan is still famous.

Next is the temple of **Degu Talle**, and then the third courtyard, the **Mani Keshab Narayan Chowk**. Restored by the Austrians, it has superb exterior decoration and a lovely central gilded window from where the kings would sit to look out over their subjects and to gaze upon the magnificent **Krishna Mandir** opposite. The octagonal *shikara*-style Krishna Mandir, considered the finest stone temple in the Valley, is pledged to be restored by the Nepal Heritage Society and is faced by a *garuda* on a column. Pause to enjoy the friezes depicting the epics that run clockwise around the building, rather like a cartoon strip. Adjacent to the Krishna Mandir is the **Bishwa Nath Mandir,** guarded by two huge stone elephants. It is one of the earlier temples in the square and is distinctive for its finely carved wood pillars.

Beyond is one of the most important temple, the **Bhimsen Mandir**, sacred to Bhimsen, the god of traders, and especially worshipped by the businessmen of Patan. From the center of the top of the three-tiered roof falls a metal ribbon-like banner engraved with mantras, donated by a wealthy benefactor.

Directly opposite, the lotus-shaped **Manga Hiti** has three stone waterspouts in the shape of crocodile heads. This Licchavi water conduit dates from the 10th century and is now well below street

Kwa Bahal - Hyranya Varna Mahabihar

level. Stand back to admire the palace façades. Return to see some interesting monuments at the upper end of the Durbar Square. **King Siddhi Narsingh** surveys the glory he has created from the top of his stone pillar, protected by a golden *naga* or serpent. The three-tiered and arcaded **Hari Shankar Mandir** acts as a visual stop to the southern end of the square. Two-tiered **Char Narayan Mandir** was built in 1566 and the octagonal stone **Krishna Temple**, which was damaged in the 1988 earthquake, was built by a Malla princess after the deaths of both her father King Yogendra Malla, and her son Lokaprakasha, to gain merit for them in their next life.

Leave the Durbar Square by the north-west corner, past some little shops, and find your way down the street to the right to the small entrance guarded by lions of the **Kwa Bahal** or **Golden Temple**, on your left. The most beautifully decorated of all the hundreds of two-storey Newari Buddhist monastery courtyards (for which Patan is renowned), this is an active and busy religious center. The entire façade of the temple enshrining the Buddha is of finely executed and lavishly embellished gilded copper.

Turn left out of the Kwa Bahal and further north is the towering **Kumbeshwar Temple**. Founded in 1392, it is the oldest in Patan and within its precincts are some early sculptures and two tanks, believed to be fed by waters from the sacred **Gosainkund Lake** high in the **Helambu** mountains. This is where the Hindu Brahmans must renew their sacred threads during the **Janai Purnima** festival in July or August. Don't miss the **Ulmanta Bhairav** shrine south of the main temple with its fine silverwork. The northern **Ashoka stupa** is just north of here in this particularly interesting and old corner of Patan. Turning right out of the temple compound follow the road left, the stupa will be visible on the left. Cross the river and you could walk to Baneswar, enjoy the view from the top of the **Everest Hotel**, then catch a cab back.

Patan Durbar Square
(a) Mul Chowk
(b) Taleju Bhawani Temple
(c) Sundari Chowk
(d) Mani Keshab Narayan Chowk
(e) Degu Talle
(f) Krishna Temple
(g) Bhai Dega
(h) Hari Shankar
(i) King Siddhi Narsingh
(j) Char Narayan
(k) Krishna Mandir
(l) Bishwa Nath Mandir
(m) Bhimsen Mandir
(n) Manga Hiti

Alternatively, return by a different route turning right to the insignificant little **Uma Maheswar**, with its beautiful 10th-century stone carving of Shiva and Parvati. Passing through the Durbar Square, turn left (east), through the bustle of the vegetable market, down a narrow brick-paved street to the large terrace square containing the **Sundhara** or golden tap. Believed to have been built to refresh the **Rato Machhendra**, it is an important stopping place for his chariot. Turn right up a paved street. At the top is the narrow entrance to the remarkable terracotta **Maha Baudha**, or the Temple of the Thousand Buddhas. Badly damaged in the 1934 earthquake, the restorers were confused by the great many parts that they could not replace, so they assembled them into another shrine in the corner. Before you leave, further down the street on the left is the famous **Uku Bahal**, a renowned courtyard with gilded roofs and a wonderful collection of metal animals. This is one of the earliest *bahals*, built in the 1650s by King Shivadeva.

2. Knives and Noses

The ridge city of Kirtipur was the last to fall to the forces of King Prithvi Narayan Shah when he unified the Kathmandu Valley in 1769.

Bicycle or drive through the rather desultory new **Tribhuvan University** buildings and climb up to the ridge-top **Newar** city of Kirtipur. The last town to fall to the forces of King Prithvi Narayan Shah during his successful conquest of the Valley in 1768 and 1769, he was apparently so enraged by the resistance and independence of the people of Kirtipur that, when he finally overcame them, he had the noses and lips cut off all the menfolk, sparing only flute players. Start by visiting the **Chilanchu Vihar** stupa which surmounts the southern hill and step around the piles of grain drying on its stone flags. Once a thriving monastery, this neglected area has four smaller stupas at cardinal points around the central stupa. Wind through the narrow medieval streets, past the ladies spinning in doorways, and the children who will offer you little dolls made from remnants of the local homemade fabric industry. The clunk of the handlooms

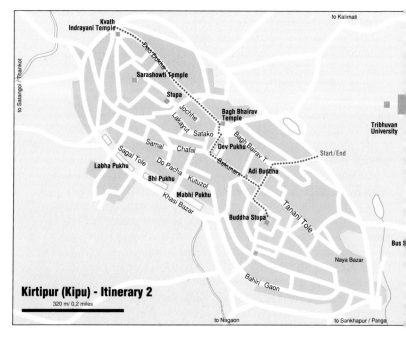

Kirtipur (Kipu) - Itinerary 2
320 m/ 0,2 miles

become a familiar sound as you pass the houses of Kirtipur.

Walking west, soon you come to a tank in the middle of the town sited below the great **Bagh Bhairav Temple**, an imposing building decorated with the daggers, swords and shields captured by King Prithvi Narayan Shah; it is a place of worship for Hindus and Buddhists alike. The **Kvath** or **Uma Maheshwar Temple** is at the highest point west of the town, guarded by two fine elephants atop a flight of steps. It commands a fine view across the whole Valley to the distant white Himalaya. Kirtipur has a forgotten feeling about it which makes it rather special, perhaps because of its independant history.

3. Shrines Sacred to Hindus

Pashupatinath and Guhyeshwari, a place of pilgrimage for the entire subcontinent.

Pashupatinath is considered one of the four most important Shiva shrines in Asia and is thus the object of many pilgrimages, especially during festivals such as **Shivaratri** when tens of thousands of devotees celebrate Shiva's birthday here in February or March. The largest temple complex in the Kathmandu Valley is so sacred that non-Hindus are forbidden to enter its most holy courtyards. There is however still much to see, not least the cremations that are almost constantly being conducted on the banks of the Bagmati, which flows eventually into the holy Ganges. To have their feet in the sacred river at the moment of death is important for Hindus to attain instant release. Two large burning *ghats* directly beneath the main temple are reserved exclusively for the royal family. Upstream there are caves, formerly used by *sadhus* or holy men for meditation, where the river twists into a gorge above the main temple.

The temple is dedicated to Pashupati, the Lord of the Beasts, an incarnation of Shiva particularly popular in Nepal. The present structure was built in 1696 on a 15th-century site by Bupalendra Malla, after the previous building had been severely damaged by termites. Like many Valley temples, the gilded copper triple roofs are decorative, and do not have corresponding floors.

The best approach is from the **Bagmati Bridge** on the Ring Road, opposite the clubhouse of the Royal Nepal Golf Club. The golf course is on land actually owned by the temple *guthi*. Having explored the shrines and

Festival of Teej

Swayambhunath Temple – shrine below stupa

sculptures in the environs of Pashupatinath, cross the two stone bridges, climb up the long flight of steps opposite and pause on the terrace to look down on the complex. At the top of the hillock is the **Gorakhnath Shikhara,** and walking on through the forest down the other side, you reach **Guhyeshwari,** the counterpart to Pashupatinath, dedicated to Shiva's *shakti*, Kali. Records of this temple complex, access to which is also forbidden to non-Hindus, date from the 17th century. Enjoy the peaceful atmosphere and if you have time, explore the edge of the river.

4. All-Seeing Eyes and a Village Shrine

Bijeswari. Breakfast at the Hotel Vajra, then up to Swayambhunath, the oldest settlement in the Valley. Finish the morning with a gentle walk to the rural temple of Ichangu Narayan.

If you are in a car, you might like to include a visit to the **National Museum** in **Chauni** (open 10 a.m. to 4 p.m., closed Tuesdays) to admire its collection of sculptures. The best direct approach is on foot from Kathmandu, about half an hour walk, crossing the river over the temporary **Vishnumati Bridge** at **Bijeswari.** Instead of following the road left, climb the steps ahead of you to the **Bijeswari Temple.**

Swayambhunath Temple –
courtyard Buddha

This Tantric shrine is especially interesting in the early morning when local people gather with their daily offerings. Stop for breakfast (or lunch) on the roof of the **Hotel Vajra,** which is situated just above the river, and enjoy the view of both the Swayambhunath Hill and over the city from this remarkable hotel. Don't miss the painted ceiling in the Great Pagoda Room at the very top of the hotel.

The magnificent setting of **Swayambhuna Stupa** dominates this area as you approach it by the tarmac road. Climb the pilgrim's route up the 300 steep stone steps on the eastern side of the forested hill, flanked with the great animal vehicles of the five Buddhas – *garudas*, peacocks, horses, elephants and lions. A huge gilded copper *vajra,* or thunderbolt, a symbol of absolute power, awaits you at the very top. The all-seeing eyes of supreme Buddhahood gaze from beneath the great gilded pinnacle with its 13 rings and crowning parasol. The nose, which looks rather like an incomplete question mark, is the Nepalese number "one", *ek*, a symbol of unity.

Mingle with monks, devout Nepalis and Tibetan pilgrims prostrating themselves full-length in reverence around the stupa that is the ancient lotus island of Manjushri's Valley lake. There is little doubt that this sacred site was established more than 2,500 years ago. Having browsed among the shrines, sculptures and monasteries, avoided the monkeys and admired the incomparable view of the Valley, leave by the west side of the hill, picking up the car at the parking place by the monastery half way up.

Head on down the hill and through the village to the Ring Road, here bordered by a wall of prayer wheels and street sellers, and strung across with fluttering prayer flags. Cross the highway, carefully, and take the dirt road directly west, past the bus station. The car, if you have one, must wait where the road peters out at a little shrine on a steep saddle. From here it is a gentle half hour walk through rice and mustard fields and past bamboo stands, cactus hedges and stone quarries to **Ichangu Narayan**, hidden in a grove of trees on the south side of the **Nagarjun Hill**.

The two-storey temple was founded, according to legend, by King Hari Datta in the 6th century but the present building is 18th century. It is one of the four important Narayan shrines that, after a period of fasting, must be visited in one day in the **Haribodhini Ekadasi** in October or November when Vishu is welcomed back from his long summer sleep. The other three are Bishankhu Narayan, Changu Narayan and Sekh Narayan.

5. Gods and Ghats

Explore the Bagmati ghats and temples of Pachali Bhairav, Tindeval, Tripura Sundari and Hem Narayan (Kalamochan). Easily **reached from behind one of Kathmandu's main arteries, this seldom-visited area reveals an intimate glimpse of daily life on your doorstep – step over the saris drying in the sun and enter another world.**

Start walking from **Tripureswar** at the small shrine of **Nav Durga** opposite the modest little Valley View Hotel. From here a dirt road leads to the holy **Bagmati River** and to the atmospheric temple of the **Pachali Bhairav**, nestled in a tabernacle within the roots of a massive *pipal* tree. This shrine, of one of the most venerated forms of Shiva, is guarded by the sleeping brass **Baital**, who is wor-

Hindu cremation rite

shipped on Tuesday and Saturday evenings and much adorned with flowers, rice and smeared with vermilion powder.

Walk on to the river, past the crumbling **Laxmeswar Shrine** on the right, where most of the courtyard has gone and much of the woodcarving is going. The charm of this area lies in its living decay. Across the footbridge are the mineral springs of the **Rajghat**.

Turn left along the Bagmati *ghats* where Hindus traditionally burn their dead, though today a cremation is more likely to be further west at **Tecko** at the confluence of the Vishnumati with the Bagmati rivers. Behind the *chaityas* and statues, is the interesting temple complex of **Tindeval**, a fine example of the Indian *shikhara* style. Nepal's religious harmony is visible in Shiva's trident standing next to Buddhist symbols of enlightenment. Walk ten minutes down the path along the river bank, past the pottery that makes decorative balustrades, and past the brick and stucco police barracks, until the imposing three roofs of the **Tripura Sundari** can be seen set back to the left within a fine courtyard. Built in 1818 by Queen Tripurasundari to increase her religious merit, the temple stands on a broad base with small temples at each corner and roof struts that depict stories from the *Mahabharata* epic.

The splendid white dome of the **Hem Narayan** or **Kalamochan,** guarded by rampant golden lions at each corner, is a little further on past a handsome red-smeared Hanuman, or monkey god, and across a small stream. This temple of obvious Moghul influence was built in 1852 by Jung Bahadur Rana to celebrate victories at war. It has a very fine statue of him set on a stone pillar and good wood-carvings. Leave the Hem Narayan by the opposite gate from the river and you are back in Tripureswar, close to **Patan Bridge**. If you want to test your reactions to the reality of 20th-century consumer society, cross the road and enter the **Bluebird Supermarket**.

6. The Late-Great Ashoka Stupas

Visit the four historically evocative stupas (the fifth central one is lost) which, if indeed erected in the third century B.C. by Emperor Ashoka, the Mauryan king of northern India, make Patan the oldest Buddhist city in the world.

You will need a car or taxi for this unusual circuit of ancient stupas, which are neither equidistant from the center of Patan nor occupy cardinal points of the compass. However they are immensely evocative with their origins shrouded in legend. Except for the

Life on the street: Tamans woman washes her reluctant son

47

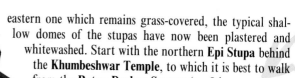

eastern one which remains grass-covered, the typical shallow domes of the stupas have now been plastered and whitewashed. Start with the northern **Epi Stupa** behind the **Khumbeshwar Temple**, to which it is best to walk from the **Patan Durbar Square** (see Itinerary 1). Returning to the Durbar Square, drive east through the winding narrow streets of the eastern outskirts of Patan to the Ring Road. Straight across, the eastern **Teta Stupa** (my favorite) stands forgotten amidst fields on the left of the little-used road to **Lubhu**.

Follow the Ring Road south; instead of taking the route left at the crossroads to **Godavari**, turn right. After a short distance is the southern **Laghan Stupa**. The top is supposed to be the only point in the Valley where you can see Mount Everest. Go on down the road. You pass on the left the extensive buildings of the Patan Hospital and on your right the outskirts of Patan. To reach the fourth western stupa, turn right at the zoo roundabout at **Jawalakhel**; look out for the Narayani Hotel as you go down the hill and the **Pulchok Stupa** is opposite on the left. Explore behind it and climb to the restored **Akshyashore Mahavihar** on an early Licchavi site.

7. Follow the Rato Machhendra

Breakfast or lunch at the Himalaya Hotel, then visit Patan, Jawalekhel and the country to the 16th-century villages of Khokana and Bungamati, winter home of the Rato Machhendra.

Enjoy the view and the food from the **Base Camp coffee shop** or by the pool at the **Himalaya Hotel**. On foot, turn left out of the hotel and keep left through Patan Gate and into the old part of the city. Skirt the Durbar Square and head south to one of the most popular temples in Patan, the **Rato Machhendranath Temple**, dedicated to the powerful Tantric deity who guards the Valley and worshipped as the god of rain and plenty. His beautiful temple stands in an open square and has intricately carved doorways and struts, and graceful windbells lining the metal roofs.

The **Rato Machhendra** is paraded every summer in a huge chariot during the festival of **Bhoto Jatra** which culminates at **Jawalakhel**. The exact month is fixed by astrologers, and a sacred bejewelled waistcoat, or *bhoto*, supposedly belonging to the serpent king, is displayed in the presence of the royal family. The chariot is then dismantled, except once every 12 years (the next occasion is in 1991) when the chariot is dragged to the Rato Machhendra's second residence at **Bungamati**, a village three miles (five km) south down a steep and rugged road. This is a difficult task undertaken very seriously because, it is said, if the chariot fails to reach Bungamati within a certain time, the god will be taken to Bhaktapur.

You may wish to visit the **Kathmandu Zoo** with its man-eating

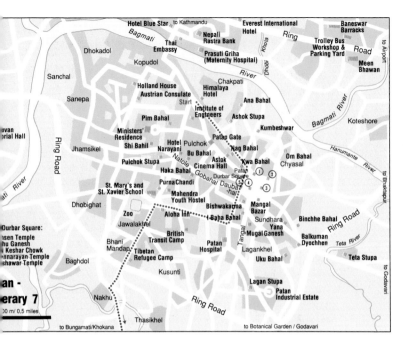

tiger brought from Chitwan. It is said that the Kathmandu Zoo is in itself a museum of sad Victorian (Rana) zoo conditions.

Explore the good Tibetan carpet shops around the **Jawalakhel Refugee Camp** and call in to watch them being dyed and woven in the traditional manner. Handmade carpets are Nepal's biggest export industry after tourism and their production employs over 100,000 Nepalis in the Valley. Turn right at the big tree to the painting shop of the artist **B.B. Thapa,** who sells charming Nepal views in the primitive style of the Sherpa and Tibetan tradition.

Take a taxi or have your car meet you here and, crossing the Ring Road, take the processional route, lined with votive *chaityas,* to the twin settlements of **Bungamati** and Khokana. Visit the *shikara*-style **Rato Machhendranath Temple**, where the powerful deity has spent his winter months since 1593, carried here most years from Patan in a simple palanquin except for the marathon when the huge chariot must negotiate this road. Visit the image of Bhairav in his nearby **Lokeshwar Shrine**.

From Bungamati it is a short walk to **Khokana**, but be sure to detour uphill to the important Ganesh shrine of **Karya Binayak** in a pretty forest clearing. The single-storey temple is in a walled compound and is often busy with families requesting help from the accommodating elephant god, Ganesh, who specialised in completing difficult tasks. There is a beautiful view from this peaceful rural shrine across the yellow mustard fields to the western foothills. When you reach Khokana, seek out the mustard oil presses for which this village is famous and the **Shekali Mai** shrine, dedicated to one of the Valley's nature goddesses.

8. Manjushri's Gorge and Kali's Sacrifice

Excursion to Chobar, Pharping and Dakshinkali, by car or bicycle, visiting the temples in this historic corner of the Valley.

If you are planning to bicycle, take a packed lunch as Dakshinkali, the furthest point, is 14 miles (22 km) from Kathmandu.

Stop first at **Chobar** where, legend tells us, the god Manjushri released the Valley lake by smiting a gorge with his sword. The Bagmati River indeed drains the Valley through a narrow gorge which slices through the Chobar Hill, though today this natural wonder is much disfigured by a belching cement factory. It is hard to ignore the results of its pollution as you climb up the steps to the **Adinath Lokeswar**, a triple-roofed Buddhist temple built in 1640 and decorated with numerous household implements: water vessels, cooking pots and pans. A metal suspension bridge spans the gorge, imported from Scotland in 1903.

Just south is the riverside shrine of **Jal Binayak,** honoring a massive rock **Ganesh**, where people who seek strength of character, worship. Also enshrined here is the thunderbolt said to have been hurled at the Valley wall by Krishna in the alternative version of the legend of the lake. The road south passes the small **Taudaha Lake,** created by Manjushri, according to legend, to house the *nagas* (serpents) stranded when the Valley was drained.

Several miles past Chobar, it would be very interesting to make a detour down a rough road to the left to the **Leprosy Commune**, now an inspiring and thriving rehabilitation centre. The 125-year old isolation barracks are slowly being replaced. Look for the sign on the tree and the yellow and red clinic at the village of **Chalnakhel**.

Follow the twists and turns of the river, with the bulk of **Champadevi Hill** looming on the right, and eventually the road reaches the lovely town of **Pharping**, just outside the Valley at an

Chobar Gorge – mountain biking

altitude of 5,148 ft (1,570 meters). The rock temple of **Sekh Narayan** honors Vishnu and stands above a series of pools full of fish, a place of pilgrimage since the 15th century. Further up the same hill is the thriving Tibetan Buddhist monastery and meditation center at the **Gorakhnath Cave**, a place of contemplation sacred to the Tibetan saint, Guru Padma Sambhava, whose footprints, carved on the platform, are dated 1390. Above Pharping is the 17th-century temple of **Bajra Yogini**, not be confused with the Sankhu temple of the same name. The Tantric goddess' pleasant visage belies her awesome instruments, a chopper with a *vajra* handle and skull cap.

Pilgrim at Dakshinkali shrine

Several miles below Pharping is the shrine of **Dakshinkali**, or southern Kali, by the bottom of a flight of stairs in a dark natural recess at a confluence between two forested hillsides. The goddess's insatiable appetite is appeased by twice-weekly sacrifices, Saturday and Tuesday, when the blood of male goats and chickens bathe the black stone image of Kali, the consort of Shiva in her most terrible form. The headless carcases are transformed into picnics for the faithful on the grassy slopes above this sinister spot. The simpler shrine of Kali's mother is a short climb up a hill beyond the lower temple.

9. The Eye of the Needle

Walk from the Godavari road to the temple of Bishankhu Narayan. Beware, as only those pure of sins can fit through a (rather narrow) cleft in the rock. Visit the Royal Botanical Garden at Godavari before returning.

Leave early in the morning to enjoy the view of the mountains, the activity in the fields and the village life through which you pass. Carry a packed meal or snack to avoid going back early for lunch.

Taking the radial road to **Godavari** from the Ring Road, pass through the villages of **Harisiddhi** and **Thaibo**, reminiscent of a Bruegel masterpiece in their symphony of colors and textures. At the end of the next town, **Bandegaon**, take the dirt road northeast. Leave the car at the first village road to await your return and enjoy walking through this magical corner of the Kathmandu Valley.

The road climbs to a saddle from which, on a clear morning, you can see as far west at the white peaks of the **Annapurna** range, north of Pokhara. The temple of **Bishankhu Narayan** is little more than a natural cave at the top of a steep stairway, but it is one of the most celebrated Vishnu shrines in the Valley. According to legend, Shiva once hid here from the demon, Bhasmasur, who had the power to turn all living things into dust and ashes at his touch. Vishnu convinced the demon to touch his own forehead and the demon turned himself to dust; the hillock adjacent to the cave is said to be made of the ashes of Bhasmasur.

After returning to the car, drive on to the village of **Godavari** where the marble quarry scars a hillside on the right. Above you is the highest hill on the rim of the Valley, **Phulchoki** (9,062 ft/2,762 m), which is a lovely place for early morning birdwatching and for spring walks in the rhododendron forests.

The first boarding school in Nepal was opened in Godavari in 1951 by American Jesuits, who still run one of the finest schools in the Valley. Father Moran, the legendary principal and ham radio enthusiast, welcomes seriously-interested educators as visitors. He was the first of very few foreigners who have been granted Nepali citizenship. Pass beneath the tall trees and you will see the stone buildings of the school set back on your right. Follow the road down the hill to the **Royal Botanical Garden**, well worth a visit and a good place to linger, except on Saturday when its peace is shattered by the mandatory stereos that accompany every party of picnickers.

10. Flight to Enchantment

A favorite not to be missed – the Royal Nepal Airlines Mountain Flight.

Royal Nepal Airlines flies east from Kathmandu for one hour every morning along the snow white peaks of the Himalaya to view the

Kongchenjunga from the air

mighty **Mount Everest** (29,028 ft/8,848 m). The highest mountain in the world bestrides the Nepal-Tibet border, and is known as Sagarmatha (Mother of the Universe) in Nepal and as Chomolungma (Mother Goddess) in Tibet. With characteristic local charm, you are normally invited to photograph, or simply to marvel, from the cockpit. Lifting even the most jaded of spirits, this flight to enchantment is an opportunity to enjoy the subtle colors of the intricate cobweb of terraced hillsides of the Mahabharat, or middle hills, as well as to glory in the awesome heights and unbelievable ranges of the highest chain of mountains in the world. Book early, and hope for crystal clear weather.

Nepal, Top Of The World

A mecca for mountaineers, climbers and trekkers, Nepal has eight of the ten highest mountains in the world and eight of the world's fourteen 26,250 ft (8,000 m) peaks within or on its borders. They are:

1. **Everest** (Sagarmatha, Chomo-lungma) in the Himalaya range on Nepal-Tibet (China) border — 29,028/8,848
2. **K-2** (Chogari, Qogir; sometimes called Mt. Goodwin Austin, but this name is not officially recognised) in the Karakoram range on the Pakistan-China border — 28,251/8,611
3. **Kangchenjunga** Himalaya, Nepal-India border — 28169/8,586
4. **Lhotse** Himalaya, Nepal-Tibet border — 27,940/8,516
5. **Makalu** Himalaya, Nepal-Tibet border — 27,766/8,463
6. **Cho Oyu** Himalaya, Nepal-Tibet border — 26,906/8,201
7. **Dhaulagiri 1** Himalaya, Nepal — 26,795/8,167
8. **Manaslu** Himalaya, Nepal — 26,781/8,163
9. **Nanga Parbat** Hindu Kush, Pakistan — 26,657/8,125
10. **Annapurna 1** Himalaya, Nepal — 26,545/8,091
11. **Gasherbrum 1** Karakoram, Pakistan (Hidden Peak) — 26,470/8,068
12. **Broad Peak** Karakoram, Pakistan — 26,401/8,047
13. **Xixabangma** (Sisha Pangma, Gosainthan) Himalaya, Tibet (China) — 26,398/8,046
14. **Gasherbrum 11** Karakoram, Pakistan — 26,362/8,035

Mount Everest from Gokyo Ri

Day Trips

11. A Goddess and a Golf Course

Explore the old trading town of Sankhu and the shrine of the Bajra Yogini. Return for lunch and in the afternoon, enjoy the facilities at the Gokarna Safari Park.

Arrange a car for the day or bicycle the 12 miles (19 km) to the sleepy town of **Sankhu**, in the northeast part of the Valley, a his-

torical stop on the old trading route to Tibet. After investigating the town, follow the road that continues only a little way north beyond the town and becomes a wide path, paved with stone. The important temple to the mysterious goddess **Bajra Jogini**, is a climb up a steep flight of steps hidden among tall dark pines. She is portrayed in a fine gold *torana* above the door of the three-roofed structure; notice the roof struts with figures of various deities. The neighboring **Gunvihar Temple** has an interesting *chaitya*. There are other shrines and sculptures in the **Bajra Yogini Dyochhen**, further up the hill. Legend has the Tantric goddess residing here from primeval history, and she is credited with having persuaded Manjushri to drain the Valley lake.

Rejoin your car in Sankhu and return down the road for lunch in the restaurant just in front of the entrance at **Gokarna Safari Park,** also known as the **King's Forest.** You will have to park the car outside, unless you are playing golf, and pay a nominal entry fee. Spend the afternoon in this pleasant setting, best avoided on weekends with its crowds of diplomatic golfers and local picnickers.

You can choose from a pretty but tricky nine-hole golf course, rent a horse for riding, or explore the forest on foot or from the back of an elephant. It is a pleasant trot in their pony and trap, but watch you don't get hit on the head by a golf ball. You are very likely to see almost-tame *chital* (spotted deer) and black buck wandering on the fringes of the forest and there are some captive tigers in a huge cage. Bird watching is good in the forest here, especially if you linger until late afternoon or stop off in the early morning.

Do a clockwise round of prayer wheels at **Bodhnath**, which you will pass on the way back. Remember, it is most auspicious to circumambulate an odd-numbered of times, and always clockwise, keeping the stupa on your right.

12. A Tantric Temple and a Shiva Screen

A bicycle ride (or arrange a car for the day) through the southern Valley towns of Sunakothi, Thecho, Chapagoan and Lele visiting the temples of Vajra Varahi and Tika Bhairav.

Turn off the Ring Road and head south at the turning marked with a red sign to the Leprosy Hospital at Anandaban, just west of the Godaveri turning – be careful as some local maps are misleading. This will be an enchanting rural day in a little-known corner of the Valley. You will enjoy the terraced green rice and yellow mustard fields, scarlet poinsettias and spikey brown cactus in the hedgerows, with always the chance of wide views of the white mountains behind.

The road passes through the 16th-century town of **Sunakothi** but you might be tempted to stop a while in the next, more friendly, settlement of **Thecho.** The **Balkumari Temple** overlooks a square used for drying golden grain and red chillies, and plenty of clamoring children. A mile (1.6 km) on is the pleasant old town of **Chapagoan**, where the surfaced road deteriorates to dirt. There are some erotic carvings on the **Bhairav Shrine** in the village. Follow the path east out of the town to the important Tantric site of the **Vajra Varahi Temple**, in a grove of sacred trees. Naturally shaped stones are worshipped here as images of Ganesh, Bhairav and the Ashta Matri-kas and on the edge of the trees are some old cremation grounds.

Returning to the main road south, there is a particularly good place to eat your picnic lunch, with fine views and shady trees, if you

apagon - Lele Valley

can find it, high above the left side of the road on a corner just before it drops down into the **Lele Valley**. Visit the eye-opening **Leprosy Hospital** in the village of **Anandaban**, which is well marked with red and white signs.

If you have the energy to continue on down the deteriorating road, be sure to look for the **Tika Bhairav** shrine to the right of the road on the edge of the village of **Lele**. It is not a temple in any conventional sense. Look for a huge brick wall, 10 by 20 ft (three by six meters) painted with a wonderful, monumental abstract close-up of Bhairav, Shiva in his most terrible form. Lele is beyond the edge of the Valley and the drive to this remote corner is well rewarded with unspoiled countryside.

13. Sleeping Vishnus and Awakening Emissaries

Balaju Vishnu and the 22 Water Spouts. Drive to Kakani. Walk to Budhanilkantha and see the sleeping Vishnu before returning.
Arrange a car and driver for the day and start by visiting the Licchavi **Balaju Reclining Vishnu** and the **22 Water Spouts**, the largest *hiti* in the Valley and always busy with people washing and bathing. They are in the small park on the left in the town of **Balaju**, just across the Ring Road northwest of Kathmandu. At the foot of the forested **Nagarjun Hill**, a favorite place for bird watchers and picnickers, this is a special little corner, very popular with locals, though avoid the public swimming pool.

Drive on past the main entrance to the Nagarjun forest and wind up the Trisuli road for about one hour (18 miles/29 km) through the terraces and bamboo stands. At the very top, turn sharp right to **Kakani**, a small village perched high on the rim of the Valley.

Kakani has a large police training school and a wonderful view. Enjoy it from the garden of the **Taragaon Hotel** and peek over the barbed-wire fence at the original Raj-style bungalow that has belonged to successive British emissaries since 1850.

At that time the British Resident's movements were greatly restricted, even within the Valley, which he was forbidden to leave, and this property was given by Jung Bahadur Rana himself as their own private retreat. Carried up by servants or arriving on ponies with their own personal army bodyguards, here the first foreign residents of Nepal could relax uninhibited by the formalities of 19th-century court life. They were free to play golf or hunt for barking deer, *chukor* partridge or pheasant, signalling when in need of further supplies to their Kathmandu Residence by heliograph, a complicated system of flashing mirrors which relied on line of sight.

Leave the car, and be sure the driver knows you wish to be met beside the great Vishnu at Budhanilkantha. Set off northeast along the line of the ridge towards the fruit farm, then seek local advice to find the trail that bears east around the flanks of the **Shivapuri**

Budhanikantha – sleeping Vishnu

Hills – the highest peak is 8,963 ft (2,732 m).

Resist the temptation to go down to your right or you will end up back in Balaju. It can be warm on this south-facing hill so be sure you carry adequate drinking water. Follow the trail for about four hours, picnicking on the way, and enjoy the wonderful view south over the entire Kathmandu Valley.

Eventually you will reach the village of **Budhanilkantha** which is close to the vanished Licchavi town called Thatungri Dranga. Pass the brick-built compound of the British-subsidised secondary school, where the Crown Prince was a former pupil, and visit the ancient **Reclining Vishnu**.

The largest and most powerful of all the four Vishnus in the Valley, this massive Licchavi sculpture is of a black stone that must have been dragged from far beyond the Valley. Lying on a bed of huge coiled *nagas* or serpents, a forecast of death forbids the kings of Nepal, themselves incarnations of Vishnu, from looking at the monumental image. Recent restaurants have sadly felled the *pipal* tree which shaded the image and imprisoned it behind concrete bars. From here it is a only a six-mile (nine-km) drive to Kathmandu.

14. Pavilioned in Splendor

Long day hike from Dhulikhel, via Nama Buddha, to Panauti.
This is a good five-hour walk and nearly two hours' drive in total, so leave Kathmandu latest by 8.30 a.m. after a good breakfast. Carry a daypack with a waterbottle and a packed lunch. You will need a car to drop you at **Dhulikhel**. Ask the driver to pick you up at about 3 p.m. from **Panauti** and ask him to wait by the **Brahmayana Temple** at the confluence of the rivers.

Turn right into the town of Dhulikhel, then left past the new buildings and government offices in this regional headquarters. Start walking up a wide well-worn trail and soon the climb reaches a little shrine and you are rewarded by spectacular mountain views extending as far west as the **Annapurnas** and even **Dhaulagiri** on a good day. Asking people as you go and skirting the jeep track, it will take you about three hours to reach the gleaming white stupa of **Nama Buddha** on the **Namara Hill**. It is a lovely, varied walk through fields and forests with constantly delightful views and, at one point, a rather alarming landslide.

Explore the prayer-flag-bedecked stupa, small monastery and newly-donated *mani* wall. Important to Tibetan Buddhists, this sacred spot is where, according to legend, the Lord Buddha offered himself to a starving tigress and her cubs. You will see this selfless incident depicted in an enshrined panel.

Eat lunch with a 360 degree view on the very highest point before dropping down on the western side of the hill to the little settlement of **Namara**, with its Swayambhunath-like stupa and huge prayer-wheel. The trail descends fairly steeply through sacred forests, then meanders through villages and cultivated fields along a very pretty valley. Be sure to note some remarkable Ganesh shrines and fine woodcarvings on the **dharmasala**s, or travelers' resthouses, in the villages on this pilgrims' route. This is quite the most impressive approach to **Panauti**, and the artistic jumble of temple roofs clustered at the **Pungamati Confluence** gleam pleasingly in the sun. Be sure to find the energy to explore this fascinating town (see Day 2) with its very early and precious temples.

Right, Namo Buddha area

Overnight Stays

Overnight Stays Outside the Valley

Despite the density of the richness of Kathmandu Valley, the real wealth of Nepal can only be appreciated by a visit to the mountains, rivers and jungles beyond the Valley. Nepal is compact, so that the diversity intrinsic in this beautiful country can be experienced and enjoyed in a condensed series of well-planned overnight visits.

Nepal is criss-crossed with trails and trade routes, making it ideal for trekking trips of four days to four weeks or more. Trekking requires not only time, but an enjoyment of camping and walking, as there are inevitable ups and downs in the Himalayan terrain, and flat ridge walking is relatively rare. If you go with a reputable agent, trekking is a luxurious experience when compared with western backpacking. Not only are there porters to carry all but a light daypack, but tents are erected, tables and stools provided and meals cooked by an unfailingly cheerful team of Sherpa guides.

Nepal's road network is less comprehensive, so without the time or desire to trek, these suggestions are necessarily restricted to driving and flying. Roads provide reliable accessibility, minimise flight delays and you can experience the wide variety of terrains in comparative comfort. The routes below will give you a feel of Nepal. Combine them as you please; link them into a longer trip, or choose one if your time is short.

15. River Running

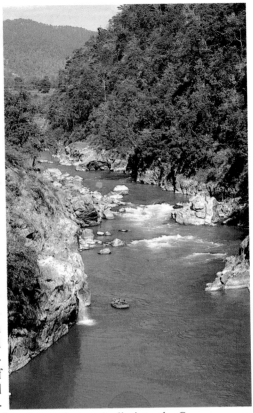

Drive early down the Pokhara road to the Trisuli River. Spend the day river running in rubber rafts, riding the rapids and enjoying the scenery at the leisurely speed of the river. Camp overnight on a white beach. The next day, continue down the river, then drive back from Mugling, through the foothills to Kathmandu.

Several huge river systems drain the Himalaya, tumbling from the heights of Tibet fed by milky glaciers, racing past the terraces of the middle hills until they slow down, through the **Terai** lowlands and meander eventually into the Ganges. The middle stretches of these rivers with evocative names such as the **Bheri**, the **Karnali**, the **Kali Gandaki**, the **Seti**, the **Sun Kosi**, the **Dud Kosi** and the **Arun** can take days and even weeks to run.

With the advantage of both convenience and accessibility, a two-day trip on the **Trisuli River** offers a lovely opportunity to experience the joys of rural Nepal at the relaxed pace of the river.

Choose a reliable operator, and they will make all the arrangements for a fixed cost. This will include securing a river permit, arranging the car, providing the boat and a trained crew, all meals and all camping equipment. I recommend **Himalayan River Exploration** (P.O. Box 170, Kathmandu. Tel: 418-491; Telex: 2216; Fax: 221-379), who pioneered the industry of river running in Nepal, maintain stringent safety standards and offer the best facilities.

The road climbs out of the early-morning Valley past the town of **Thankot**, the earth-satellite station and King Tribhuvan's polite wave. With clear skies, the first glimpse of **Himalchuli** (25,896 ft/ 7,893 m) and **Manaslu** (26,781 ft/8,163 m), will take your breath away as you reach the rim.

The main road to India drops down to the truck-stop village of **Naubise**, where it divides. Branch right and on through the hills until you get to the put-in point at the village of **Kuringhat**, where you bump down to the river over sculptured stones.

The comfortable rubber boats are supported by a rowing frame and piloted by an experienced oarsman. Your personal belongings are stowed in black waterproof bags and sealed ammunition boxes. Although always within reach of the road, the river trip travels self-sufficient of camping gear, food, drink and helpers to assist in both rowing and camping, as well as interpreting the sights and sounds of the riverside villages and the flora and fauna of the riverbanks.

Pausing at a wayside shrine, exploring a simple settlement or waving at curious children, a day on the river is hard to beat. Between the adrenalin rush of the rapids, all with alluring names and some of which change with the seasons, the flat, calm stretches provide ample opportunity for swimming, relaxing and reflecting. Unusual trees and flowers, colourful birdlife and the ever-changing scenery combine with the peaceful river sounds to produce a mood of mixed excitement and contentment. Sleep in tents on the sand beaches after an evening around a driftwood fire.

The river trip ends early afternoon of the second day, when the imposing bridge at the roadside town of **Mugling** comes into view. Here the road divides to **Pokhara** (a three-hour drive) or to **Narayanghat** (one hour). It is about three hours' drive back to Kathmandu. If there is time, another day floating on the river brings you to beautiful and majestic **Royal Chitwan National Park** (see Itinerary 17 for a full description).

16. Magnificent Mountains

The verdant Pokhara valley is 124 miles (200 km) west of Kathmandu. The old trading bazaar of Pokhara is beneath the towering Annapurna Himal, dominated by the distinctive peak of Machhapuchhre, the sacred Fishtail. Stay for one or two nights by the lakeside to enjoy the sleepy atmosphere and the stunning views.

Take a half-hour flight from Kathmandu west to **Pokhara** along the mountains, sitting on the right side of the aircraft for the best view. Driving takes six hours, and longer if you detour to the restored 15th-century palace and temple of **Gorkha**, seat of King Prithvi Narayan Shah, who united Nepal in 1768 and founded the present dynasty. Ideally, drive there from Kathmandu, and fly back.

Set in the wide, lush, green valley of the **Seti River**, the old trading town of Pokhara sprawls over several miles. Decorated pony trains from the Kali Gandaki trade routes jostle with men from the mountains bartering in the bazaar. Busses hoot and trekkers stride down the street *en route* for the hills.

More peaceful is the **Phewa Lake**, south of the airstrip and the main town. On a clear morning the snowy outlines of the **Annapurna Himal** and the unmistakable **Fishtail** peak of **Machhapuchhre** are reflected in its depths. This is the place to enjoy the restful atmosphere of this almost tropical valley of Nepal. *Jacaranda*, banana and papaya trees flourish at this altitude of about 3,000 ft (900 m).

If you want to do more than relax, there are day walks to **Sarankot** and **Naudanda,** or much more interesting is to walk up towards **Kalikathan** on the first day of the Royal Trek or explore the pretty valley beyond **Lake Begnas**, east of Pokhara. Tourists visit the **Mahendra Caves** and the **Henja Tibetan Camp** but more fun is the **Tibetan Camp** at Parde and Devi's Fall, where the river disappears underground into a sinister hole. Keen birders should visit the fascinating **Pheasant Farm**, (strictly by appointment only. Tel: 061-20039), belonging to the legendary Colonel Jimmy Roberts, "father of trekking". Donations are welcome for the World Pheasant Association projects in Nepal.

Sunrise at Phewa lake, with Annapurna III and IV, and Machhapunchhre in the background

Depending on your budget and mood, choose to stay in the **Fishtail Lodge** (Tel: 061-20071 but book well in advance. P.O. Box 140, Kathmandu. Tel: 221-711; Telex: 2205; Fax: 225-236), which has an unrivalled position by the lake but mediocre service. Better value is the **Hotel Mount Annapurna** (Tel: 061-20027/20037) across from the airport with good roof-top views. This modest Tibetan managed hotel has charming murals. Also recommended is the scrupulously clean **Gurka Lodge**, run by an ex-officer and his British wife, Shirley. The hotel is behind the lake opposite the Fishtail Lodge, there are only four lovely rooms in a secluded garden.

17. Jungle Jaunt

In one of the most beautiful wildlife areas in Asia, Tiger Tops has been operating memorable trips to this former hunting reserve well before it became Royal Chitwan National Park. Choose from a combination of nights at the world-famous Tiger Tops Jungle Lodge, the Tented Camp for wildlife devotees or the Tharu Village Resort for a unique mix of luxury and village life on the edge of the jungle.

It is a half hour's flight every day in a Twin Otter aircraft to Tiger Tops' **Meghauly** grass airstrip, where you are met and escorted by landrover or elephant across the **Rapti River** and into **Royal Chitwan National Park** (360 sq miles/967 sq km). This airstrip was extended at the visit of Queen Elizabeth II in 1961, for what was to be one of the last of the great tiger hunts in this historic region, where royalty and viceroys had been hosted for decades by the rulers of Nepal. Tiger Tops can also be reached by a five-hour drive from Kathmandu or Pokhara, or a three-day trip down the river.

The survival of the **Terai** wildlife of Nepal was threatened when the endemic malaria was eradicated in the 1950s, and large numbers of hill people settled in the Chitwan valley, clearing the forest habitat for cultivation. Chitwan is at an altitude of 450 ft (140 m). The fear of an unknown Nepal, malaria and fever had effectively acted as a southern blockade, deterring potential invaders and isolating the few indigenous Tharu people who had developed a partial resistance to the disease.

Safari tents

One-horned Indian rhinos

Gazetted in 1972, this beautiful park was first set aside to protect not the magnificent **Royal Bengal tiger**, but the **Greater One-Horned rhinoceros** whose prehistoric bulk, with its characteristic folds of skin, thrives in the tall grassland areas of the lowland **Terai**. Once hunted for its lucrative horn valued by the Chinese for medicinal properties, poaching is now virtually unknown.

Another important endangered species found in the Narayani River is the **Gharial crocodile**, with its long narrow snout developed for catching fish. The wildlife of Chitwan is rich and diverse, with over 450 species of birds, including all the summer migrants and winter visitors.

The elephant grass grows to 25 ft (eight m) in height and makes the domestic elephant an essential and practical means of conveyance. Some species of the mixed riverine forest include the *bombax*, or silk cotton tree, with its red blossom and later white cotton which showers the forest floor, and the brilliant orange flame-of-the-forest. The tall *sal* trees (*shorea robusta*), with their large, flat leaves grow on higher ground in the **Siwalik (Churia) Hills**, the last wave of the Himalaya along the Indian border. Also, this part of the park is the home of the elusive **gaur**, largest of the world's wild cattle.

Tiger Tops (P.O. Box 242, Kathmandu. Tel: 222-706; Telex: 2216; Fax: 221-379) will show you the glories of Chitwan, from the elegant tree-top rooms of **Tiger Tops Jungle Lodge** in the heart of the park, or from the comfort of the **Tented Camp** on a plateau commanding views across the whole width of Nepal. The knowledgeable naturalists' guide walks and landrover-drives through the forest, visits to *machans* (hides) overlooking *tals* (small lakes) and boat trips down the Rapti and Narayani rivers. The best part is to ride the

Machans, or blinds, for wildlife viewing

elephants in search of wild animals, or to bathe with them in the river at the elephant camp.

First opened in 1964, Tiger Tops pioneered controlled eco-sensitive tourism with its solar energy, wildlife research programmes and educational services for the local communities.

The **Tiger Tops Tharu Village**, set in a beautiful wild garden on the edge of the park, offers a combination of more general wildlife and cultural activities and is open all the year round. The spacious rooms are styled after Tharu longhouses, decorated with artefacts and mud paintings; there is a swimming pool, nightly local dancing and a stable of horses and ponies on which to explore the surrounding countryside and villages.

18. Wildlife Wonders

Royal Bardia National Park, in far west Nepal, is the favored destination for the true wilderness enthusiast, rich in all the wildlife of the subcontinent. The four-hour drive from Nepalgunj to Tiger Tops Karnali Lodge and Tented Camp is through virgin forest and colorful Tharu villages.

Providing you have at least three nights and a real interest in wild places, it is worth making the extra effort required to get to **Royal Bardia National Park**, reached by air via the **Terai** town of **Nepalgung** in the far west. Due to its easy accessibility, Chitwan is in danger of overcrowding, whereas the 373 sq miles (968 sq km) of Bardia remain untouched.

The main attraction is the variety of bird and animal life, including the wild elephant, swamp deer, black buck, blue bull and ghoral that do not occur in Chitwan. Baiting is still permitted in Bardia, making it one of the best places to see the **Royal Bengal tiger**. Also

Sunset on the Karnali River

Karnali Lodge

found are the **leopard, rhinoceros, sambar, chital, wild boar, Rhesus** and **Langur monkeys, Gharial** and **Marsh Mugger crocodiles** and **Gangetic dolphins**.

This part of the western Terai is the home of the most interesting and colorful group of **Tharu**, the collective name given to the original animistic people who farm, hunt and fish in the *duns* (valleys) of Nepal's lowlands. Adorned with magnificent silver jewelry, brilliantly colored skirts and navy-tattooed ankles, the proud women of the Dangaura Tharu live in unique longhouses. Accommodating as many as 30 families and their livestock, these intriguing mud buildings shelter under huge grass roofs and owe little to the modern world. Divided into rooms by large moulded vats of grain, the inhabitants' belongings hang in baskets from the roof.

Explore the forests and *phantas* (short grasslands) of this beautiful national park by elephant, jeep and on foot, and travel by boat on the massive **Karnali River,** which spills out through its narrow gorge onto the plains of the Terai. One of the great wilderness experiences for the intrepid traveler is the four-day white-water trip down the **Bheri River**. Fishing for **mahseer**, the mighty sport fish of the Himalaya, is at its best in February and March when the snow-fed waters are clear. Photographed and weighed, the catch is then released to fight another day.

All arrangements are made by **Tiger Tops** (P.O.Box 242, Kathmandu. Tel: 222-706; Telex: 2216; Fax: 221-379), for booking the 45-minute flight to Nepalgunj where you are met and escorted the four-hour drive through the villages and jungles to Bardia. Your daily programme is discussed with you on arrival. **Tiger Tops Karnali Lodge**, with its soaring timber and thatch roofs, elegant terraces and twelve comfortable rooms, is on the edge of the park, adjacent to the Tharu villages. The **Karnali Tented Camp** stretches along the banks of the Karnali River, tucked away within the forest and evoking days of the Raj with its spacious safari tents and attentive service, all the more appreciated for being in this remote sanctuary.

Fishing for *Mahseer*

Sun Kosi Gorge, on the way to Tibet

19. A Walk on the Wild Side

Drive to the Tibet border town of Zhangmu (Khasa) and stay overnight in the Zhangmu Hotel. Drive up the gorge to Nyalam, through the Himalayan range and onto the Tibetan plateau. Cross two spectacular passes amidst rugged, arid terrain to Tingri for a wonderful view of the mountains, including the peaks of Everest and Cho Oyu, now astonishingly seen from the north. Return to Khasa for the night. On the following day return to Kathmandu, stopping for lunch at the Dhulikhel Mountain Resort.

It must be stressed that this is a tough trip due to the altitude and can be very difficult to operate owing to a number of circumstances. The Chinese visa regulations for Tibet are subject to change, but at the moment are only granted to a group of at least four, and require several days' stay in Kathmandu; secondly, the Chinese, who do not permit vehicles to cross the border, may not be able to supply vehicles of their own; and thirdly, the road between Kathmandu and the Tibetan plateau is not infrequently blocked by either landslides (in summer) or snow (in winter). Even if all these conditions are favorable, the cost of the venture may deter some travelers.

You may wonder why I have included it at all. The reason is that, despite these deterents, this trip is so stunning, the variety of scenery so spectacular and the change in cultures and climes so extraordinary that I would urge anyone who has the opportunity to move heaven and earth to give it a try.

Start by checking all the various imponderables with your travel agent in Kathmandu (**Adventure Travel Nepal**, P.O.Box 242, Kathmandu. Tel: 223-328; Telex: 2216; Fax: 221-379). Make sure you have a re-entry visa to Nepal as well as a Chinese visa for Tibet. Equip yourselves with warm clothes, as the winds on the arid Tibet

plateau will be cold throughout the year. Take sunglasses, suncream and scarves to protect yourself from the glare and the dust. Take extra food and chocolate to sustain you in case you don't like what the hotel offers.

Take Diamox, a diaretic drug which helps the body acclimatize to altitude. Although in one day's drive you go from Zhangmu at 6,930 ft (2,112 m), to the highest pass over 16,000 ft (5,000 m), because you descend back to sleep at Zhangmu that night, there really is no danger. However, you may suffer temporary symptoms such as giddiness, headaches and nausea – Diamox helps dispel these. Take plenty of liquid to drink (not alcohol) and move slowly and cautiously in the high, thin air.

The drive on the **Arniko Highway** to the border takes about four hours and is very beautiful, winding through the terraced hills and the great valleys of the **Sun Kosi River** and its tributary, the **Bhote Kosi**. Set off early, armed with a packed lunch, and be prepared for delays at the border.

You pass through the Nepali towns of **Barabise** and **Tatopani** noting remnants of landslides. Nepal immigration is at **Kodari**, and soon after, the first Chinese soldiers on the **Friendship Bridge** come into view.

The no-man's-land between the Nepal checkpost and entry into Tibet on the edge of the sprawling trading depot of **Zhangmu** (known confusingly as **Khasa** in Nepal) is a steep hillside above the Bhote Khosi. The miserable **Zhangmu Hotel** is immediately after the checkpost on the left. Also confusing is the fact that Chinese time is three hours and fifteen minutes ahead of Nepalese time.

Leave as early as you can the next morning and be prepared for one of the most extraordinary days of your life. There is something magical about leaving the lush Nepalese alpine scenery, penetrating the Himalayan range through the spectacular, deep gorge of the Bhote Kosi, and emerging into another world, that of ancient Tibet. You are now in the rain shadow, north of the white peaks of the great mountains that only yesterday you had seen from the south. Guarded by ruined *dzongs* (forts), the arid plateau is tilled by yaks, while nomads herd their sheep and goats, and the medieval villages of Tibet huddle against the harsh glare of the elements.

North of the small town of **Nyalam,** perched at the head of the gorge, is the village of **Zhonggang** and the recently rebuilt cave monastery of **Phenkyeling**. This is said to be one of the cave retreats of Milarepa, the 11th-century hermit. The road climbs across two passes, the **Thong La** (16,303 ft/4,970 m) and the **Lalung La** (16,665 ft/5,050 m), crowned with stone *chortens* (cairns) and prayer flags, proffered in thanks for a safe journey.

The drama of the vista of the multi-colored mountains unfolds in a memorable panorama. **Xixabangma** (26,398 ft/8,046 m), also known as **Gosainthan,** is the only 26,000-ft (8,000-m) mountain that is completely within Tibet, and can be seen to the west. After reaching the stone village of **Tingri**, you can see the north faces of **Everest** (29,029 ft/8,848 m) and **Cho Oyu** (26,906 ft/8,201 m) across the plains against a cobalt sky. From here it is another two days' drive to **Lhasa**.

After a second night at the Zhangmu Hotel, return as soon as Chinese and Nepalese border formalities can be completed. Lunch in the comparative civilisation of the **Dhulikhel Mountain Resort**, amidst the green and gold of Nepal's countryside. It is barely an hour from here back to Kathmandu – and the "real" world.

A **pleasant alternative**, if logistics and permissions to Tibet are not forthcoming, is to drive from Kathmandu down the Arniko Highway as far as you wish towards the Tibetan border. Return to spend the night in the private chalets of the Dhulikhel Mountain Resort (P.O.Box 2303, Kathmandu. Tel: 220-031; Telex: 2415; no fax) enjoying the views, walks and comfort that this charming establishment has to offer.

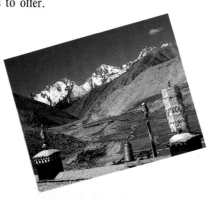

Right, a Tibetan *drukpa*, nomad

Nepali Cuisine

Unlike other Asian countries, Nepali cuisine is nothing to write home about. Based on similar principles as north Indian cooking, the ordinary people of Nepal live on rice, *dahl* (lentils), curried vegetables, and eat meat usually only during festivals. True Nepali specialities are found only in private houses, so be sure to accept an invitation if offered. It is curious that Nepal's isolation did not spawn more regional specialities, especially as the Kathmandu Valley produces such superb vegetables in its fertile fields. However, there are now several restaurants that serve Nepali food, though their menus are usually combined with Indian or Tibetan dishes.

There are a wide variety of other cuisines on offer, including Chinese, Japanese, Italian and English. Prices in Nepal are generally much lower than elsewhere. Outside Kathmandu and Patan it is difficult to find appealing food, even for a snack, so on a day outing carry something from the bakeries or Thamel delicatessens, or a packed lunch from your hotel.

Produced in Nepal are a variety of alcoholic drinks including good beer, rum, vodka and gin and more dubious whisky and brandy. Try the local *raksi* (distilled rice or wheat) or *chang* (fermented grain, usually barley or millet) if offered in a private house. Imported wines

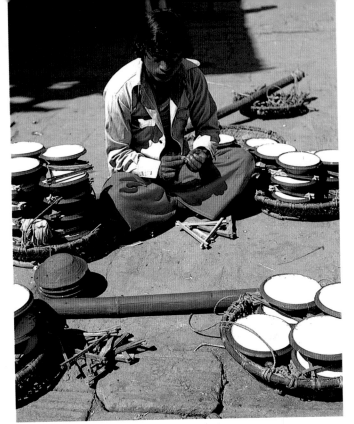

Yoghurt is sold in earthernware bowls

are available only at the hotels and better restaurants, at often prohibitive prices. Bottled soft drinks such as Coke and Pepsi, and mineral water are widely available.

A drink in the bars of Thamel before dinner is always fun to people-watch – try **Spam's Spot** for local colour and the **Rumdoodle** for trekkers and climbers. Otherwise night life is minimal, despite a couple of desultory discotheques in the hotels, and restaurants rarely stay open after 10.30 p.m. – except the only casino in the region at the **Soaltee Oberoi Hotel**, which never closes.

Nepali Restaurants

Bhancha Ghar, Kamaladi Tel: 225-172. Nepali food in a converted old house designed for tourists but with considerable charm.

Ghar E Kebab, Hotel Annapurna, Durbar Marg. Tel: 221-711. Terrific Indian kebabs and curries with live *sitar* music at night. Be sure to book ahead, as this is probably the most popular restaurant in town.

Himalchuli, Hotel Soaltee Oberoi. Tel: 272-550. Nepali and Indian specialities with a cultural show at 8 p.m. nightly.

Naach Ghar, Hotel Yak & Yeti, Durbar Marg. Tel: 411-436. Nepali and Indian food in a beautiful neo-classical ballroom with a cultural show Sundays and Tuesdays. Consider splurging, if there are more than 10 people, have the hotel arrange a special dinner in one of their amazing Rana reception rooms.

Sun Kosi, Durbar Marg. Tel: 220-299. Good traditional Nepali and Tibetan cuisine in a cosy brick interior. Ask for the homemade *achars* (chutneys).

Other Options

Al Fresco, Hotel Soaltee Oberoi. Tel: 272-550. Italian cuisine in a lively taverna atmosphere. Pizzas and desserts are especially good and the pasta in a walnut cream sauce is delicious.

Coppers, Keshar Mahal. Tel: 417-095. Try the fresh fruit drinks, steak and kidney pie and open charcoal grill specialities in this first-floor English and European restaurant, stylishly decorated in copper, wood and marble. Ask for the daily special.

Brass pots sell by the weight

Everest Hotel Roof Garden, Baneswar. Tel: 224-960. Call in for a coffee or a drink at the Gurkha Bar to enjoy the view.

Fuji, Kantipath. Authentic Japanese food in picturesque Rana cottage complete with stucco columns and moat.

Kushu Fuji, Durbar Marg, above Tiger Tops. Try the fixed lunches and watch the world go by from a window seat in this restaurant, an old favorite with the Japanese.

Mountain City Chinese, Malla Hotel, Lekhnath Marg. Tel: 410-320. The best Chinese food in town with authentic Sichuan cooks and professional service.

Mike's Breakfast, Durbar Mark, off the Yak and Yeti road. Serves huge breakfasts, soups and quiches in a charming Rana cottage garden. Good music and good value.

Yak & Yeti Hotel Sunrise, Durbar Marg. Tel: 411-436. Interesting coffee shop menu for lunch in this convenient meeting place overlooking palace gardens. Try the salad bar and Thai specialities.

Shopping

Kathmandu is a treasure trove of opportunities for shoppers, but beware of the cheap trinkets that tend to look like the junk they are when you return home. It is expected that you will bargain, except in the smart shops, and even there it is worth a try. As a general rule, if you like it and can afford it, buy it – you may never find the same thing again. The main shops are in **Thamel, Durbar Marg** and **Jawalakhel** but you will find temptations wherever you go.

Nepal Handicrafts

One very positive boon of the tourist boom is the improvement in locally made handicrafts. For a wide selection of what is available under one roof, call in at **Hastakala** (Handicrafts) opposite the Himalaya Hotel in Patan. All the crafts on sale in this attractive shop are made in Nepal by disadvantaged groups; proceeds go to charity.

Look out for handspun fabrics from Kirtipur, brass candlesticks from Patan, woodcarvings in the form of traditional window photo frames and beautiful handmade paper and cards from Bhaktapur. The **Mahaguthi** shops, one just down the hill in Patan and one in Durbar Marg have similar arrangements. **Pasal**, in an arcade off Durbar Marg, sells especially clever gift items of imaginative local and regional decorative items, household goods and toys.

Thangkas

Beautiful religious scroll paintings hung in silk are best bought in Bhaktapur where they are painted. Look in the shops in **Tamaudi Tole** leading down from the Durbar Square, check for fine detailed work and gold leaf. Also look in the **Indra Gallery** in Thamel. Multi-colored masks and dancing puppets can be found in Bhaktapur. Check out the terracotta animals at Thimi although you must be very dedicated to hand-carry them home. Patan craftsmen are famous for their metalwork, and silver and goldsmiths ply their trade using tools and methods unchanged for centuries. Especially interesting is the "lost wax" method of casting bronze which can be seen at **Nepal Traditional Crafts** (Tel: 521-071) in Patan on the right up the hill past the Himalaya Hotel.

Nepal Carpets

Now a major export industry, these beautiful handmade wool carpets are world famous and good value in Nepal, as you might expect. Choose from the wide selection from the shops in **Jawalakhel**, or Thamel. Mostly three by six feet (one by two meters) in traditional Tibetan designs, the soft pastel colors are very popular, though not 'natural dyed' as they would have you believe.

Pashmina Shawls

Wool and mixed wool shawls are available from shops in Thamel but the best selection is from **Everest Pashmina Arts** in Kamal Pokhari (opposite the old Lhotse Hotel). Made from the finest goat wool, the pure white ones are the most expensive.

Jackets and Sweaters

Less fine but quite fun are the multi-colored sweaters available in Thamel. Patchwork jackets sold in the Yak and Yeti Hotel road are amusing and the wool waistcoats and crossover jackets made from the monk's wool cloth in **Bodhnath** (in a shop on the west side of the stupa) are wonderful.

Silk

Nepal silk is not yet up to international standards but be tempted by the delightful hand-painted Chinese silk outfits and scarfs in **Mandala** and **Tara**, elegant boutiques in Durbar Marg and Keshar Mahal respectively.

Gurkha Khukris

The genuine *khukris*, traditional curved knives of Nepal, are for sale in the **Tiger Tops shop** in Durbar Marg, hand made by British Gurkha soldiers in their army workshops. Beware of poor-quality imitations being sold on the streets.

Jewelry

No major precious stones are found in Nepal but you will find good silver-work bracelets and tiny animals in the traditional Nepali filigree designs, sometimes inlaid with small corals or turquoise.

The Sherpas and Tibetans value the dark red coral highly. Turquoise should be bright blue-green. Both are traded from Tibet and are not cheap. Look for pretty silver bangles and earrings; unique to Nepal are the plaited bangles of three metals – copper, brass and silver (or iron) – popular with those who suffer from arthritis. Most convenient are the **Durbar Marg** or **New Road jewelers**. Try the excellent **Gem Palace** at the Yak and Yeti Hotel or **Noor Gems** near the Woodlands Hotel in Durbar Marg for a selection of what is available. Enjoy making up your own combinations of multi-colored glass beads in the **Bead Market**, tucked away in Indrachowk.

Paintings

B.B.Thapa, in his shop to the right beside the big tree opposite SATA in Jawalakhel, offers an enchanting range of Kathmandu Valley and Nepal views in the primitive style normally associated with the Sherpa or Tibetan fresco painters. He also has a selection on the road outside the Soaltee Oberoi.

Antiques and Art Objects

Kathmandu is a treasure trove for collectors. Glory in a galaxy of superb old Tibetan carpets, precious *thangkas*, Chinese embroideries, porcelain and jade, Bhutanese dress pieces, coral and turquoise jewelry, gold and silver ritual art objects and fine Nepali bronzes.

It is no longer easy to find bargains and prices tend to be index-linked. Be aware of the local restrictions for exporting, which require certificates for some antiques; get the shopkeeper to help you. Recommended: the **Tibet Ritual Art Gallery** and the **Potala Gallery**, on first floors in Durbar Marg and the **T. T. Gallery** below Coppers Restaurant in Keshar Mahal but keep your eyes open in Bodhnath.

By appointment only call **Barbara Adams** (Tel: 417-617) to see her beautiful collection of antiques and ethnic fabrics for sale in her home in Naxal.

Calendar of Special Events

Nepal is known as the land of festivals. Here, in the shadow of the mountain gods, colorful celebrations are so frequent that the festivals often overlap each other. There are more than 50 such occasions a year, with as many as 120 days set aside to be observed. Nepalis celebrate enthusiastically, and you are welcome to take part.

Festival dates vary from year to year because of the lunar calendar. Many are determined only after complex astrological calculations and as some festivals take place over a period of several days, it is usually difficult to know in advance which day festivities will take place, or where. The uncertainty is even considered part of the mystery.

This list will give you a guideline, but you must be sure to check when you arrive in Kathmandu. Remember, the dates given below may change. Consult the daily newspaper first.

Magha
(January and February)

Magha Sankranti. Marked with ritual bathing, even though it often falls on the coldest day of the year, this festival marks the passing of the inauspicious winter month of Pousch and rejoices that spring is at hand.

Maha Snan. Celebrates the holy bath given to Shiva, when he is bathed in yoghurt and honey and dressed anew.

Basanta Panchami. *January 21, 1991*. The Festival of Spring is also the festival of Saraswati, goddess of learning. Students about to take exams and hundreds of devotees flock to the Saraswati shrine at Swayambhunath. The King attends ceremonies at Hanuman Dhoka to offer prayers for a good harvest. A most auspicious day to get married or to introduce children to the alphabet.

Magha Purnima. *January 31, 1991*. The full moon (*purnima*) marks the beginning of the month in which Parvati must be worshipped at her shrines.

Falgun
(February and March)

Democracy Day or King Tribhuvan Jyanti. *February 18, 1991*. The statue of King Tribhuvan is garlanded in a procession to Tripureshwar on this holiday.

Shivaratri. *February 13, 1991*. This great festival celebrating the birthday of Shiva is the time to be at Pashupatinath.

A colorful crowd of literally thousands of devotees, *yogis* and *sadhus*, or holy ascetics, from all over the Indian subcontinent gather to line up to make offerings to Lord Pashupati, keep a night time vigil with bonfires and bathe at dawn in the holy Bagmati River.

Bodhnath – New Year Festival

Losar or Tibetan New Year. One of the most beautiful festivals, usually coincides within a few days of Chinese New Year. The third day of the otherwise family and house-oriented holiday is the time for celebrating at Bodhnath. Everyone dresses in their best clothes and jewelry and joins in the celebrations at this temple where new prayer flags are hung, the Dalai Lama's portrait paraded and one of the great moments of the year takes place as hundreds of Tibetans throw *tsampa* or barley flour into the air accompanied by a great roar of welcome to the New Year. Dancing takes place in the evening at monasteries around the stupa at Bodhnath.

Holi. *March 1, 1991.* Kathmandu Durbar Square is where this rowdy festival of color and fertility is celebrated with the raising of a 25 foot *chir* or bamboo pole, bedecked with streamers, which is burned at the end of the week. Wherever you are, wear old clothes as you are likely to be sprayed with colored water by enthusiastic kids.

Chaitra
(March and April)
Seto or Rath. For four days during early evening, the guardian deity of the Seto (White) Machhendra is pulled in a towering chariot through the streets of Kathmandu before being returned on a small palanquin to his shrine in Asan.

Ghorajatra. Celebrated by horse races and gymnastics attended by the King, this horse festival has become a military pageant and draws crowds to the Tundekhel.

Pase Chare. Coincides with Ghorajatra. After the horsemanship displays, the demon Gurumpa is carried to the Tundikhel in a midnight procession.

Chaitra Dasain. *March 24, 1991.* Ritual offerings and sacrifices are made to Durga, exactly six months away from her great festival of Desain.

Baisakh
(April and May)
Bisket. Bhaktapur is the place to be for this exciting and rowdy festival which lasts for a week and celebrates the slaying of two demon serpents. A frenetic tug of war at dusk by men of the town determines who shall have the honor of dragging a huge chariot conveying Bhadrakali and Bhairav through the streets. Spectacular masked dancing and the felling of a long pole, commemorating victory during the great battle of Mahabharata, mark the beginning of the Nepalese New Year.

Seto Machendranath Festiv

Bal Kumari Jatra. The New Year is marked at Thimi with torch-lit processions honoring the Bal Kumari, a consort of Bhairav.

Matatirtha Aunshi or **Mothers Day.** Persons whose mothers have died during the year must ritually bathe near Thankot. Living mothers are offered gifts.

Buddha Jayanti. As Nepal is the birthplace of Lord Buddha, his birthday is celebrated with great veneration at all Buddhist shrines, particularly Bodhnath and Swayambhunath.

Jesth
(May and June)
Sithinakha. Jaisedewal, south of Kathmandu Durbar Square, will be thronged with people celebrating the birthday of Kumar, son of Shiva. Today rice planting begins and wells must be cleaned and their serpent inhabitants tended.

Asadh
(June and July)
Tulsi Bijropan . This women's festival of fasting and purification involves planting the sacred *tulsi* plant, a close relative of common basil.

Gokarana Aunshi or Fathers Day. *June 30, 1991.* This festival is celebrated by ritual bathing at the Gokarna Mahadev for those whose father has died in the past year. Living fathers are also honored with gifts and sweets.

Srawan
(July and August)
Bhoto Jatra. Astrologers fix the exact time. The culmination of the months' long procession of the Rato (Red) Machhendranath chariot since it set off from Pulchok in April, this important Patan festival is designed to ensure a good monsoon rainfall for crops.

The bejewelled waistcoat or *bhoto*, supposedly belonging to the serpent king, is displayed at

Jawalakhel in the presence of the royal family. Once every 12 years (the next time is 1991) the chariot is dragged all the way to Bungamati.

Ghanta Karna. The Night of the Devil is traditionally the last day for rice planting. The demon was outwitted by a frog and children collect coins to pay for his funeral.

Naga Panchhami. *August 14, 1991. Nagas*, or the sacred serpents, are worshipped and pictures can be seen displayed above many doorways.

Raksha Bandhan or Janai Purnima. Every Brahman and Chhetri must renew their *munja*, or sacred thread, on this day after first taking a ritual bath in holy water.

The Kumbeshwar Temple in Patan is the place to be, as the water in the tanks there supposedly come from the sacred Gosainkund Lake, high in Helambu. The beautiful gold and silver *linga*, usually kept in the temple, are displayed on this day on a platform in the middle of the tank, reached only along a narrow plank.

Gai Jatra. An epic love of a king and queen is celebrated in this festival, which is more like a carnival. Families in which deaths have occurred in the previous year will send cows or children dressed as cows to frolic and sing in the Durbar Squares of Kathmandu, Patan and Bhaktapur to assist their deceased's entry into heaven.

Gai Jatra – masks make men gods

Krishna Jayanti. Birthday of the beloved god Krishna is celebrated in Patan Durbar Square.

Badra
(August and September)
Teej. This colorful women's festival has groups of red sari-clad ladies singing in high spirits in the streets on their way to ritually bathe in the Bagmati River at Pashupatinath.

Indrajatra. Probably the most spectacular of all Valley festivals, torch-lit processions and dancing to honor Indra, the god of rain, in this eight-day celebration which centers on the Kathmandu Durbar Square. On the third day the *Kumari*, the Living Goddess

is paraded in a special chariot and worshipped by the King himself. Masks of Bhairab decorate the city and local beer pours forth from their mouths to refresh the local revellers.

Ashwin
(September and October)
Dasain or Durga Puja. This ten day festival is celebrated all over Nepal, honoring fertility and the conquest of evil. Normal life comes to a standstill as everyone attends their religious and family duties.

On *Phulpati*, the day of flowers, there is a colorful procession to Hanuman Dhoka attended by the King. On the eighth and ninth days there are massive numbers of ritual animal sacrifices, for every tool that is used during the year must be blessed. Shrines all over the country literally run with blood. On the final day the palace is opened for all who wish to line up to receive a *tika* from the hands of the King or Queen.

Kartik
(October and November)
Tihar, or Diwali, and Lakshmi Puja. *November 5, 1991.* The Festival of Lights starts with honoring the crow, the dog and the cow. The fourth day coincides with Newari New

Pashupatinath - Teej

Year and there is much merriment, gambling and feasting. On the fourth and fifth evenings Laksmi, the goddess of wealth and prosperity, is enticed into the home by lights. The towns glow with thousands of oil lamps and candles adorning doors, windows and balconies. Walk through the Durbar Squares and bazaars to enjoy these prettiest nights of the year. Brothers are feted by their sisters on the last day and honored with elaborate *tikas* and garlands.

Haribodhini Ekadasi. This most auspicious *Ekadasi* (the eleventh day of each lunar fortnight, there are 24 in a year, strictly observed by fasting) welcomes Vishnu back from his long summer sleep. Join worshippers at Budhanilkantha or, better still, follow pilgrims as they visit all the four great Narayan temples in the Valley in one day, each at least 10 miles (16 km) apart.

HM The Queen's Birthday. *November 8, 1990 and 1991.* The Queen receives a procession of well-wishers who visit the palace up Durbar Marg.

Marga
(November and December)
Yomari Purnima. The Newari rice festival is celebrated at Panauti, where the family paddy store is blessed and special rice cakes are prepared.

Poush
(December and January)
Constitution Day or **King Ahendra Jayanti.** *December 16, 1990* and 1991. Garlands are laid on the statue of King Mahendra in Durbar Marg.

HM The King's Birthday. *December 29, 1990 and 1991.* Durbar Marg is the place to watch the colorful parade bursting with well-wishers who bring birthday greetings and offerings to the King on this holiday.

Prithvi Jayanti. The statue of King Prithvi Narayan Shah opposite Singa Durbar is garlanded and his photograph paraded through the city.

TRAVEL ESSENTIALS

When to Visit

The winter months are the best time for a visit, from October to April. October and November days are sunny and clear. However, being the most popular, this is also the most crowded time. The cold clear winter months of December and January are good for mountain views, despite misty mornings and an invigorating evening chill.

Next busiest, and in many ways the best, months are February and March with spring flowers and gentle temperatures. Late April and May can be hot and hazy and it is best to avoid the monsoon rains from June to September if you are planning to trek or visit the lowland national parks.

In the Valley, however, this can be one of the prettiest times with intermittent rain, lush green rice fr wonderful light effects and very other visitors.

Visas

Visas valid for 15 days can be bo on arrival at Kathmandu airport US$10 by all foreign nationals ex British passport holders, for whom fee is £20. Be sure you have pass sized photographs and the right ch to avoid delay.

Visas valid for 30 days can be tained from a Nepalese Embassy to arrival. All tourist visas can be tended at the Department of Immi tion in Thamel, Tel: 412-337 (ope a.m. to 5 p.m. daily but Friday un p.m., closed Saturday) for up to t made in foreign exchange by foreigners. American Express and Visa cards are widely accepted.

months, upon proof that at least $10 per day has been exchanged for duration of the visa.

you are planning to leave and re-, be sure to ask for a multi-entry. k permits must be obtained by visi- planning to trek or travel to areas er than the Kathmandu Valley, hara or the Terai.

accinations

accinations against typhoid, hepati- (gamma globulin) and meningitis recommended. Make sure your rou- tetanus and polio inoculations are to date. Yellow fever vaccinations essential if arriving from an infected a. Cholera shots are neither required recommended.

Money Matters

Nepalese rupees are the monetary t and the official rate of exchange ctuates against other currencies. In e 1990 the rate was Rs 29.20 to $1 but check the *Rising Nepal*, ere rates are published daily on the k page.

Money can be changed in the banks hotels and the exchange counter at airport. Beware of the black market hard currency is in high demand. ep all Foreign Exchange Encashment ceipts as these are necessary for visa ensions and changing back excess ees on departure.

t is illegal to export or import palese currency. All airline, hotel travel agency payments must be

Clothing

Your wardrobe will depend on what you are planning to do in Nepal but generally only the most casual clothes is required. Safari-style cottons, modest skirts, jeans and comfortable track shoes are ideal with a warm sweater and jacket for cold winter evenings. Bring sunglasses for daytime and rely on a local umbrella if it rains, which is sel- dom except during the monsoon. If you are trekking or river running, consult an equipment list for specialist gear.

Electricity

Electrical outlets are rated at 220 volts/50 cycles though some fluctua- tion is not unusual. Power cuts are common. Big hotels have their own generators. A small flashlight will be quite useful.

Airport Tax

A departure tax of Rs 450 is charged per person on all international flights and Rs 30 on some (not all) domestic flights.

GETTING ACQUAINTED

Government and Geography

Nepal is a constitutional monarchy headed by His Majesty King Birendra Bir Bikram Shah Dev. Following violent demonstrations and riots in early 1990, the palace announced on 8 April 1990 the lifting of the legal ban on political parties. The Prime Minister, Krishna Prasad Bhatterai, heads an appointed Council of Ministers as an interim government entrusted with the task of preparing the new democratic arrangements.

The King (born 28 December 1945) and Queen Aishwarya Rajya Lakshmi Devi Shah (born 7 November 1949) have three children; the older, His Royal Highness Crown Prince Dipendra (born 27 June 1971) is heir to the thrown and is currently attending Eton College in England. Nepal is the only Hindu monarchy in the world.

Over 90 percent of the 19 million population of Nepal and the 50 per cent under the age of 21 growing at the annual rate of 2.6 per cent, are engaged in agriculture.

As they are subsistence farmers, industriously carving out a living from

small plots on terraced hillsides, annual per capita income of US$ looks more alarmingly low than it

Development is hampered by lac roads and infrastructure in this lar mountainous land which, in only miles (160 km) goes from the hig point on earth (Mount Everest, kn in Nepal as Sagarmatha, 29,028 8,848 m to the lowland Terai less 350 ft (100 m) above sea level.

About the same size as Englan New Zealand, Nepal stretches 553 n (885 km) from east to west and h total land area of 56,139 sq n (145,391 sq km).

Health care and literacy figures amongst the world's worst and Nep largely dependant on foreign aid fo economic development. Tourism is single largest foreign exchange ear closely followed by hand-made w carpet exports.

Kathmandu, the capital, is at an titude of 4,400 ft (1,350 m) and h population of about 500,000, with most one million people making Kathmandu Valley their home.

Climate

Nepal has an extreme variety of mates, from the eternal snows of Himalaya to the tropical lowlands. capitals enjoy as many hours of s shine as the Kathmandu Valley, wh has three seasons:

inter season

ctober to March, 10° - 25°C (50° -
F), with cold nights dropping to
ost freezing and a morning mist due
he rapidly rising daytime tempera-
s. Clear sparkling sunny days.

pring season

pril to mid-June, 11° - 30°C (52° -
F), with warm, sometimes hazy days
occasional evening thunder storms,
nights are pleasantly cool.

Monsoon season

une to September, 19° - 36°C (6° -
F), intermittent violent downpours
en only at night) create some flood-
and landslides, and keep the tem-
ature down and the humidity high.

ime

epal is five hours 45 minutes ahead
GMT and 15 minutes ahead of Indian
ndard Time.

Calendars

Five different calendars are used si-
taneously in Nepal. The official one
d by the government is the lunar
ram Sambat calendar which started
nting on 23 Feb 57 B.C. Hence 1991
2048 of the Vikram era. However,
familiar Gregorian calendar is
lely used. The traditional ones are
Newari calender, the Sakya Era
endar and the Tibetan calendar.

The Nepalese year, which begins in
d-April, is 365 days long with 12
nths ranging in length from 29 to 32
s, depending on solar movement.
ese calendar months are called:
isakh (April - May), **Jesth** (May -
e), **Asadh** (June - July), **Srawan**
ly - August), **Bhadra** (August -

September), **Ashwin** (September - Octo-
ber), **Kartik** (October - November),
Marga (November - December), **Poush**
(December - January), **Magha** (January
- February), **Falgun** (February -
March), **Chaitra** (March - April).

Hours of Business

Government offices are open from 10
a.m. to 5 p.m., Sunday through Friday,
though they close at 4 p.m. during
three winter months and early on Fri-
days at 3 p.m.

Banks open at 10 a.m. and close at 2
p.m. except Friday when they close at
12 noon. Saturday is the only rest day
in Nepal although most of the shops
remain open every day until 7 or 8 p.m.
Only embassies and international or-
ganizations have a two-day weekend.

Culture and Customs

Although every visitor is immediately
struck by the charm and smiling friend-
liness of the Nepali people, avoid inad-
vertently offending your hosts and keep
the following in mind. Both men and
women can go about almost everywhere
with confidence but keep your wallet
out of sight and your bag zipped up.

If you are approached or hassled by
the curious, smiling patiently usually
gets better results from these proud
people than losing your cool. Rarely do
people mind being photographed, but
it is polite to stop if they do.

Nepalis are on the whole very tolerant of visitors' behaviour, but respect in temples and shrines is expected – be ready to remove your shoes. The traditional greeting, *Namaste*, literally translated as "I Salute All Divine Qualities In You", should be spoken while raising the hands in a prayer-like gesture. The King is regarded with genuine reverence as an incarnation of the Hindu god, Vishnu, so all references to the royal family must be suitably respectful.

Never point with a finger and specially not with your feet, never touch the top of anyone's head and never give or receive anything in your left "polluted" hand – best is to offer and receive with both hands.

Tipping

It is customary to tip about 10 percent in restaurants, hotels and taxis, though not mandatory. Give two or three rupees to a porter who helps with your bags. What seems little to us is not insignificant when compared to local salaries. However do refrain from giving sweets and money to every child who asks.

Tourist Information and Maps

Rely on guide books; there are many. Recommended is *Cityguide: Kathmandu Valley* and *Insight Guide: Nepal*, both published by Apa Publications and widely available in the many excellent bookshops in town. The informative *Nepal Traveller* magazine may be handed to you at the airport. Erwin Schneider's Kathmandu Valley map is the best and the orange street-map of Kathmandu, published by Himalayan Booksellers, is useful.

GETTING AROUND

Private Cars

The most convenient, reliable time-effective way to get around is a private car and guide from a tr agent or hotel. If you stay within rim of the Valley, it will cost you a US$50 for the whole day. If you satisfied a Rs 50 tip is customary.

Taxis

Taxis are available to go most pl and have black registration plates v white numbers; private cars have w numbers on red plates. Make sure t meters are working and be prepare pay a 10 percent fuel surcharge.

Bicycles

A great way to see the Valley is bicycle, especially the new moun bikes, which are ideal for exploring dirt roads of the Valley. Ordinary cycles cost as little as Rs 10 a day (fr the rental shops in Asan and Than but mountain bikes are worth the ext **Himalayan Mountain Bikes** (n

amandu Guest House (Tel: 413-
418-733) offer escorted trips
nd the Valley and beyond.

alking

prepared to do a lot of walking if
wish to taste the real flavor of the
ey, absorb its people, their culture
way of life.
ost of the interesting sites have to
eached and explored on foot. Leave
main roads and stroll at a leisurely
through the rice and mustard
s. You can expect to be safe every-
re and will find the people even
e friendly off the beaten track.

ublic Transport

uses, trams, three-wheeled scooters
pos) and bicycle-rickshaws all ply
streets of Kathmandu but are gen-
ly to be avoided unless you are
ing for an ethnic experience.

WHERE TO STAY

lotels and Lodges

he prices below are for a room only
f late 1990 and do not include serv-
charges (10 percent) or government
which varies from 12-15 percent
ending on the category.
he star ratings awarded by the De-
tment of Tourism are quantitative
her than qualitative, and this list is
no means exhaustive.
hose marked with (*) officially have
star rating. There are plenty of
ges and guesthouses for less than
$10 to choose from in Thamel.

सा.वि.

Five-star

Annapurna
Durbar Marg
Tel: 221-711, 223-602
US$80 (single) US$90 (double)
Now run by the Taj Group from
India, this central hotel was the first
five-star in town.

Everest
Baneswar
Tel: 224-960, 220-389
US$100 (single) US$110 (double)
Until recently managed by Sheraton,
the best thing about this hotel is the
view from the roof.

Soaltee Oberoi
Tahachal
Tel: 272-550/5
US$95 (single) US$110 (double)
The best hotel in town, though not
conveniently located for walking,
with extensive facilities, excellent
restaurants and the most spectacular
"regal" suites built for the South
Asian (SAARC) Heads of State.

Yak and Yeti
Durbar Marg
Tel: 411-436, 228-803
US$95 (single) US$105 (double)
Excellently located, this historic
home of the great Boris Lissanevitch,
founder of Nepal's tourism, is part
Rana palace and part modern.

Four-star

Dwarika's Kathmandu Village*
Battisputali
Tel: 414-770, 412-328
US$57 (single) US$74 (double)
A wonderful Nepali antique woodcarving collection is incorporated into this imaginative family-run hotel.

Himalaya
Kupondole
Tel: 523-900/8
US$70 (single) US$85 (double)
Cool white marble, spacious rooms and a swimming pool with a view in this Japanese owned property.

Kathmandu
Maharajgunj
Tel: 410-786, 413-082
US$74 (single) US$91 (double)
This is rather cramped, with a miniscule garden, but has an interesting brick atrium architecture.

Malla
Lekhnath Marg
Tel: 410-320, 410-966, 410-968
US$56 (single) US$80 (double)
Well placed and well run, recently re-furbished. Has a charming garden and the best Chinese food in town.

Shangrila*
Lazimpat
Tel: 412-999, 410-108
US$65 (single) US$80 (double)
Lovely brick-built favorite with good food, great service and a definite plus, a glorious garden.

Shanker
Lazimpat
Tel: 412973, 410151
US$65 (single) US$80 (double)
Spectacular white neo-classical palace in huge gardens, very well placed but unfortunately not very well run.

Three-star

Crystal
New Road
Tel: 223-397, 223-611, 223-636
US$35 (single) US$45 (double)
You get a terrific view from the r● garden in this old haunt at the top New Road.

Narayani
Patan
Tel: 521-711, 521-712, 521-408
US$50 (single) US$57 (double)
In the shadow of an Ashoka stu; handy for Patan.

Summit*
Kupondole Heights
Tel: 521-894, 524-694
US$35 (single) US$49 (double)
Lovely rooms, view and swimming po● in this pleasant hotel, though not ve conveniently situated.

Yellow Pagoda
Kantipath
Tel: 220-392, 220-337
US$44 (single) US$54 (double)
Has been recently redecorated; know● for its consistent service; very centr● location.

o-star

bassador
impat
: 410-432, 414-432
$19 (single) US$22 (double)
venient. Run by the same manage-
nt as the legendary Kathmandu
est House.

ra
eswari
: 271-545, 272-719
$23 (single) US$25 (double)
re a cultural experience than a hotel,
s wonderfully off-beat hotel's lack of
lities (few adjoining bathrooms and
 telephones in the rooms) is more
n made up for by its vibrancy and
ftop bar.

e-star

e Diamond
amal Tole
: 213-392, 216-320
$7 (single) US$9 (double)
ghtly off the beaten track,
e garden, popular with ex-
ditions.

Kathmandu Guest House
Thamel
Tel: 413-632, 418-733
US$14 (single) US$17 (double)
One of the best and certainly the most
famous of the Thamel lodges. In the
heart of the action; often fully booked.

Star
Thamel
Tel: 411-004, 412-100
US$6 (single) US$8 (double)
Next door and next alternative to the
Kathmandu Guest House.

Tibet Guest House
Chetrapati
Tel: 214-383, 2158-93
US$14 (single) US$15 (double)
Friendly, helpful and excellent value,
this comes well recommended.

HEALTH AND EMERGENCIES

Hygiene

It is not uncommon for minor problems to occur and elementary hygiene
precautions are in order. Never drink
unboiled and untreated water and do
not trust ice cubes anywhere except the
best hotels. Avoid eating raw vegetables, peel all fruit and do not be
tempted to eat anywhere except proper
restaurants. Never walk barefoot and
wash your hands often. "Traveler's
Tummy" should clear up after a few
days but is it is severe and persistent, or
interferes with your travel plans, get a
stool test and medical assistance.

Medicine

Most medicines that you will require are readily and cheaply available without a prescription. Look out for the well-known brand names manufactured under license in India and check the labels carefully as contents may be different from those you are familiar with at home. Do not rely on pharmacists when making a diagnosis but get medical assistance.

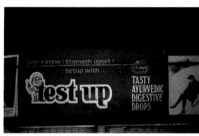

Clinics

There are Nepali doctors attached to all the big hotels. The **Nepal International Clinic** in Naxal (Tel: 412-842). Best of all is the American-staffed **CIWEC Clinic** in Baluwatar (opposite the Russian Embassy. (Tel: 410-983).

Hospitals

Some Kathmandu hospitals do have English-speaking staff but are not up to international standards; and where feasible, foreign visitors are advised to get to the excellent facilities found in Bangkok.

For accidents and emergencies, the recommended hospitals are the **Patan Hospital** in Lagankhel, Patan, (run by the United Mission to Nepal Tel: 521-034, 521-048, 522-286, 522-278) and the **Teaching Hospital** in Maharajgunj (Tel: 412-303, 412-404, 412-505, 412-808).

COMMUNICATION AND NEWS

Telecommunications and Postal Services

Main hotels have telephones, ca telex and mail facilities. Internati direct dial telephone communicat are satellite-linked and excellent. country code is 977 and the Kathma area code is 1.

If you are having trouble, dial for the international operator, 187 calls to India, 180 for internal t calls and 197 for enquiries.

The Telecommunication Office Tripureshwar deals with telephone and telexes if your hotel cannot. telex service is available only du government hours at the Central T graph office. Telefax has reached N but only in the more progressive off Ask your travel agent or hotel public service is available.

The mail service is less reliable avoid having people send you let during your visit. Mail cards or let at your hotel or at the General I Office (Tel: 211-037) at the junctio Kantipath and Kicha-Pokhari.

Parcels from abroad are received sent from the adjacent Foreign I Office (Tel: 211-073).

nant in the Kathmandu Valley, uses three different alphabets and is the richest in literature and poetry.

In northern Nepal the Tibetan language remains widespread and is the basis of dialects such as Sherpa and Thakali. English is widely spoken and understood, especially in government and tourism-related circles.

Media

There are several English newspapers d dozens in Nepali. The official Eng-h *Rising Nepal* has a smattering of eign news and devotes a lot of its nt page to the King's activities. *The ternational Herald Tribune* can be und one day late at newsstands and ailable weekly are *Time*, *Newsweek*, e *Far Eastern Economic Review*, iaweek and *India Today*.

Radio Nepal broadcasts two news lletins in English daily at 8 a.m. and 30 p.m. Nepal Television arrived in 86 and broadcasts only for five hours ery evening, with an English news at 40 p.m. Check the programmes daily the *Rising Nepal* and bring a short-ave radio if you are addicted to inter-tional news.

SPECIAL INFORMATION

Nepali Language

There are as many tongues spoken in epal as there are races and almost as nany dialects as there are valleys. The fficial language, Nepali, is derived om Pahori, an Indian language re-ted to Hindi and uses the same writ-ng system, Devanagari. Nepali has also orrowed heavily from Sanskrit, an ncient scholarly language which has urvived (like Latin) as a religious nedium. Newari, the unique ancient anguage of the Newar people predomi-

SPORTS

Other than the hotels, sports facilities are very limited for visitors, with the exception of the two golf courses that exist in the Valley, both nine holes and with browns instead of greens. Temporary members are welcome at the **Royal Nepal Golf Club** (Tel: 472-836) near the airport and at **Gokarna Safari Park** (Tel: 470-063) past Bodhnath in the King's Forest where you can even follow your round with an elephant

ride. The five-star hotels all have swimming pools, tennis courts and some have health clubs.

Leisure is a concept unfamiliar to Nepalis who traditionally spend their spare time tending to family and religious commitments.

USEFUL INFORMATION

Key Telephone Numbers

Police Emergency	226-998
Red Cross Ambulance	2280-94
Patan Hospital	521-034
	521-048
	522-286
	522-278
Teaching Hospital	412-303
	412-404
	412-505
412-808	
CIWEC Clinic	410-983
Nepal International Clinic	412-842
Fire Brigade	221-177
Telephone Enquiry	197
International Operator	186
Operator for India	187
Internal Trunk Calls	180

Credit Card Offices

American Express
Durbar Marg. Tel: 226-172

Visa
c/o Nepal Grindlays Bank
Tel: 212-683 Ext 38

International Organisations

French Cultural Center,
Bagh Bazaar. Tel: 224-326

British Council
Kantipath. Tel: 221-305

Goethe Institute
Sundhara. Tel: 220-528

International Monetary Fund
Tel: 411-977

United Nations
Pulchok. Tel: 523-200

US AID
Kalimati. Tel: 270-144

US Information Service
New Road. Tel: 223-893

USSR Cultural Center
Ramshahpath. Tel: 216-248

World Bank
Kantipath. Tel: 226-792

Airlines

Air France
Durbar Marg. Tel: 223-339

Air India
Kantipath. Tel : 212-335

Bangladesh Biman
Durbar Marg. Tel: 222-544

British Airways
Durbar Marg. Tel: 222-266

Cathay Pacific
Kantipath. Tel: 226-765

Dragon Air
Durbar Marg. Tel: 227-064

Druk Air
Durbar Marg. Tel: 225-166

Indian Airlines
Durbar Marg. Tel: 411-997

Japan Airlines
Durbar Marg. Tel: 412-138

Lufthansa
Durbar Marg. Tel: 224-341

orthwest Airlines
antipath. Tel: 226-139

akistan International
urbar Marg. Tel: 332-102

an American
urbar Marg. Tel: 225-292

oyal Nepal Airlines
ew Road. Tel: 220-757

ingapore Airlines
urbar Marg. Tel: 220-759

wissair
urbar Marg. Tel: 222-452

hai International
urbar Marg. Tel: 225-084

rans World Airlines
antipath. Tel: 226-704

ravel Agencies

dventure Travel Nepal
urbar Marg. Tel: 223-328

nnapurna Travels & Tours
urbar Marg. Tel: 223-940

verest Express
urbar Marg. Tel: 220-759

orkha Travels
urbar Marg. Tel: 224-896

athmandu Travels & Tours
angapath   Tel: 222-985

alla Travels
alla Hotel. Tel: 410-635

arco Polo
amal Pokhari. Tel: 414-192

Natraj Tours & Travels
Tel: 222-014

Shankar Travel
Shankar Hotel. Tel: 422-465

Tiger Tops
Durbar Marg. Tel: 222-706

Trans Himalayan Tours
Durbar Marg. Tel: 224-854

World Travels
Durbar Marg. Tel: 226-939

Yeti Travels
Durbar Marg. Tel: 221-234

Trekking Agencies

Above the Clouds Trekking
Thamel. Tel: 416-923

Amadablam Trekking
Lazimpat. Tel: 410-219

Asian Trekking
Keshar Mahal. Tel: 412-821

Himalayan Adventures
Lazimpat. Tel: 411-477

Himalayan Journeys
Kantipath. Tel: 226-626

Himalayan Rover Trek
Naxal. Tel: 412-667

International Trekkers
Durbar Marg. Tel: 220-594

Journeys Mountaineering & Trek king. Tel: 225-969

Lama Excursions
Durbar Marg. Tel: 220-186

Mountain Travel Nepal
Naxal. Tel: 414-508

Natraj Trekking
Kantipath. Tel: 226-644

Nepal Trekking
Thamel. Tel: 214-681

Sherpa Cooperative Trekking
DurbarMarg. Tel: 224-068

Sherpa Trekking Service
Kamaladi. Tel: 222-489

Trans Himalayan Trekking
Durbar Marg. Tel: 223-854

Foreign Missions in Nepal

Australia
Bhat Bhateni. Tel: 411-578

Bangladesh
Naxal. Tel: 414-943

Burma
Pulchok. Tel: 521-788

China
Baluwatar. Tel: 411-740

Egypt
Pulchok. Tel: 521-844

France
Lazimpat. Tel: 412-332

Germany (East)
Dilli Bazaar. Tel: 214-801

Germany (West)
Kantipath. Tel: 221-730

India
Lainchaur. Tel: 410-900

Israel
Lazimpat. Tel: 411-811

Italy
Baluwatar. Tel: 412-743

Japan
Pani Pokhari. Tel: 414-083

Korea (North)
Patan. Tel: 521-084

Korea (South)
Tahachal. Tel: 211-172

Pakistan
Pani Pokhari Tel: 410-565

Thailand
Thapathali. Tel: 213-910

USSR
Baluwatar. Tel: 412-155

United Kingdom
Lainchaur. Tel: 410-583

USA
Pani Pokhari. Tel: 411-179

FURTHER READING

There are a number of very good bookshops in Kathmandu with an excellent selection of the varied books on Nepal. These include: **Himalayan Booksellers** with branches in Durbar Marg, Kantipath, Thamel; **Pilgrims Book Centre** in the depths of Thamel; **Educational Enterprises** in Kantipath opposite Bir Hospital; **Himalayan Book Centre** in Bag Bazaar; and the **Tibet Book Store** in Keshar Mahal beneath Coppers Restaurant.

General

Hagen, Toni. *Nepal: The Kingdom in the Himalayas.* Berne: Kummerly and Frey, 1980.

Geographical study with many photos and maps. Hagen spent eight years surveying Nepal, mostly on foot. He's one of the first persons to travel widely in the country. This book is still one of the best.

Van Gruisen, Lisa. *Insight Cityguide: Kathmandu Valley.* Apa Publications, Singapore, 1990.

In-depth survey of history, culture and detailed descriptions of monuments and temples in the Kathmandu Valley.

Peissel, Michel. *Tiger for Breakfast.* Hodder, London, 1966.

The story of Kathmandu's legendary Boris Lissanevitch, who first came to Kathmandu in 1951 and opened the first hotel, the Royal.

Suyin, Han. *The Mountain is Young.* Jonathon Cape, London, 1958.

Charming novel capturing the heady atmosphere of Nepal in the 1950s.

People, art and culture

Anderson, Mary M. *Festivals of pal.* George Allen & Unwin, Lon 1971.

Best summary of festivals.

Aran, Lydia. *The Art of Nepal.* hayogi Prakashan, Kathmandu, 1

Mostly about the Kathmandu V with an accent on religion.

Bista, Dor Bahadur. *People of N* Ratna Pustak Bhandar, Kathma 1974.

Classic survey.

Kuloy, Hallvard Kare. *Tibetan.* Bangkok: White Orchid Press 198

Nicely illustrated paperback the scanty information.

Natural history

Fleming, R.L. Sr, R.L. Flemin and L.S. Bangdel. *Birds of N* Avalok, Kathmandu, 1979.

Definitive work, good illustratie

Hillard, Darla. *Vanishing Tra Four Years Among the Snow Leopar Nepal.* Arbor House, New York, 1

A charming study of life in the v ern Himalaya with zoologist Ro Jackson.

Inskipp, Carol. *A Birdwatcher's G to Nepal.* Bird Watchers Guides, I land, 1988.

Excellent and helpful guide.

McDougal, Charles. *The Face of Tiger.* Rivington Books and A Deutsch, London, 1977.

Classic work on the tiger by Wildlife Director of Tiger Tops.

lunin, Oleg and Stainton, Adam. *ise Flowers of the Himalaya.* OxUniversity Press, New Delhi, .

much-needed standard work with tiful illustrations.

nith, Colin. *Butterflies of Nepal tral Himalaya).* Teopress, Bang- 1989.

holarly standard work.

orrs, Adrian & Jimmy. *Enjoy s: A simple guide to some of the bs found in Nepal.* Sahayogi Press, hmandu, 1987.

seful and practical handbook.

rekking

ezruschka, Stephen. *A Guide to king in Nepal.* The Mountaineers,

Seattle, 1981.

Probably the best trekking guide, written by a doctor with personal experience in Nepal.

O'Connor, Bill. *The Trekking Peaks of Nepal.* Seattle: Cloudcap Press 1989 and England: Crowood Press.

Excellent and detailed guide with useful maps.

Swift, Hugh. *Trekking in Nepal, West Tibet and Bhutan.* Sierra Club, San Francisco, 1989.

Good general route information.

Van Gruisen, Lisa. *Insight Guide: Nepal.* Apa Publications, Singapore 1990.

Most complete coverage of trekking, climbing, national parks and the Terai, and something on Kathmandu Valley.

GLOSSARY

A

Ananda	The Buddha's chief disciple.
Ananta	A huge snake whose coils created Vishnu's bed.
arak	A whiskey fermented from potatoes or grain.
Asadh	The third month of the Nepalese year (June-July).
Ashwin	The sixth month of the Nepalese year (September-October).
Ashta Matrikas	The eight mother goddesses said to attend on Shiva.
Avalokiteshwara	A *bodhisattiva* regarded as the god of mercy in Mahayana Buddhist tradition, and as the compassionate Machhendra in Nepal.
avatar	An incarnation of a deity on earth.

B

bahal	A two-storey Buddhist monastery enclosing a courtyard.
bahil	A Buddhist monastery, smaller and simpler than a *bahal.*
Baisakh	First month of the Nepalese year (April-May).
Bajra Jogini	A Tantric goddess.
betel	A stimulating mixture of areca nut and white lime, wrapped in a betel leaf and chewed.
Bhadra	The fifth month of the Nepalese year (August-September).
Bhagavad-Gita	The most important Hindu religious scripture, in which the god Krishna spells out the importance of duty. It is contained in the *Mahabharata.*
Bhairav	The god Shiva in his most terrifying form.
Bhimsen	A deity worshipped for his strength and courage.
bodhisattiva	In Mahayana tradition, a person who has attained the enlightened level of Buddhahood, but has chosen to remain on earth to teach until others are enlightened.
Bon	The pre-Buddhist religion of Tibet, incorporating animism and sorcery.
Brahma	In Hindu mythology, the god of creation.
brahman	The highest Hindu caste, originally made up of priests.

C

Chaitra	The 12th and last month of the Nepalese year (March-April).
chaitya	A small stupa, sometimes containing a Buddhist relic, but usually holding *mantras* or holy scriptures.
chang	A potent mountain beer of fermented grain, usually barley but sometimes maize, rye or millet.
chhetri	The Hindu warrior caste, second in status only to *brahmans*.
chiya	Nepalese tea, brewed together with milk, sugar and spices.
chorten	A small Buddhist shrine usually in high mountain regions.
chowk	A palace or public courtyard.
crore	A unit of counting equal to 10 million.

D - F

Dalai Lama	The reincarnate high priest of Tibetan Buddhism and political leader of Tibetans around the world.
Dattatraya	A syncretistic deity variously worshipped as an incarnation of Vishnu, a teacher of Shiva, or a cousin of the Buddha.
Devi (or Maha Devi)	"The great goddess". Shiva's *shakti* in her many forms.
dhal	A lentil soup.
Dharma	Buddhist doctrine. Literally 'the path'.
dharmasala	A public rest house for travelers and pilgrims.
dhoko	A basket, often carried on the head by means of a strap.
dorje	A ritual sceptre or thunderbolt, symbol of the Absolute to Tantric Buddhists (also *vajra*).
Durga	Shiva's *shakti* in one of her most awesome forms.
dyochhen	A house enshrining protective Tantric deities and used for common worship.
Falgun	The 11th month of the Nepalese year (February-March).

G - H

gaine	A wandering, begging minstrel.
Ganesh	The elephant-headed son of Shiva and Parvati. He is worshipped as the god of good luck and the remover of obstacles.
Garuda	A mythical eagle, half human. The vehicle of Vishnu.
Gautama Buddha	The historical Buddha, born in Lumbini in the 6th century B.C.
ghat	A riverside platform for bathing and cremation.
gompa	Tibetan Buddhist monastery.
Gorakhnath	Historically, an 11th-century yogi who founded a Shaivite cult; now popularly regarded as an incarnation of Shiva.
guthi	A communal Newar brotherhood, serving the purpose of mutual support for members and their extended families.
Hanuman	A deified monkey. Hero of the *Ramayana* epic, his is believed to bring success to armies.
hiti	A water conduit; a bath or tank with water spouts.

I - J

Indra	The god of rain.
Jagannath	Krishna, worshipped as "Lord of the World".
jatra	Festival.
Jesth	The second month of the Nepalese year (May-June).
jhankri	A shahman or sorcerer.
jogini	A mystical goddess.
jyapu	Newar farmer caste.

K

Kali	Shiva *shakti* in her most terrifying form.
karma	The cause and effect chain of actions, good and bad, from one life to the next.
Kartik	The seventh month of the Nepalese year (October - November).
kukhri	A traditional knife, long and curved, best known as the weapons of Gurkha soldiers.
Krishna	The eighth incarnation of Vishnu, heavily worshipped for his activities on earth.
kumari	A young virgin regarded as a living goddess in Kathmandu Valley towns.

L

lakh	A unit equal to 100,000.
Lakshmi	The goddess of wealth and consort of Vishnu.
lama	A Tibetan Buddhist priest.
lingum (plural:*lingas*)	A symbolic male phallus, generally associated with Shiva.

M

Machhendra	The guardian god of the Kathmandu Valley, guarantor of rain and plenty, who is enshrined as the Rato (Red) Machhendra in Patan and the Seto (White) Machhendra in Kathmandu.
Magha	The 10th month of the Nepalese year (January - February).
Mahabharata	An important Hindu epic.
Mahayana	A form of Buddhism prevalent in East Asia, Tibet and Nepal.
Maitreya	The future Buddha.
mandala	A sacred diagram envisioned by Tibetan Buddhists as an aid to meditation.
mandap	a roofless Tantric shrine made of brick or wood.
Manjushri	The legendary Buddhist patriarch of the Kathmandu Valley, now often regarded as the god of learning.
mantra	Sacred syllables chanted during meditation by Buddhists.
Marga	The eighth month of the Nepalese year (November-December).
math	A Hindu priest's house.
munja	The sacred thread worn by *brahman* and chhetri males from the time of puberty.

N

naga	Snake, especially a legendary or a deified serpent.
namaste	A very common word of greeting, often translated as: "I salute all divine qualities in you".
Nandi	A bull, Shiva's vehicle and a symbol of fecundity.
Narayan	Vishnu represented as the creator of life.
nath	literally, 'place'.
nirvana	Extinction of self, the goal of meditation.

P

panchayat	A government system consisting of elected councils at local, regional and national levels.
Parvati	Shiva's consort, displaying both serene and fearful aspects.
pashmina	A shawl or blanket made of fine goat's wool.
Pashupati	Shiva in his aspect as 'Lord of the Beasts'. Symbolized by the *lingum*, he is believed to bring fecundity.
path	A small raised platform which provides shelter for travelers on important routes and intersections.
paubha	Traditional Newari painting, usually religious in motif.
pokhari	A large tank.
Pousch	The ninth month of the Nepalese year (December-January).
puja	Ritual offerings to the gods.

R

rakshi	A homemade wheat or rice liquor.
Rama	The seventh incarnation of Vishnu. A prince of the *Ramayana* epic.
Ramayana	The most widely known Hindu legend, in which Rama, with the aid of Hanuman and Garuda, rescues his wife, Sita, from the demon king Rawana.
Rawana	The anti-hero of the *Ramayana*.
rimpoche	The abbot of a Tibetan Buddhist monastery.

S

sadhu	A Hindu mendicant.
sanyasin	A religious ascetic who has renounced his ties to society.
Saraswati	Brahma's consort, worshipped in Nepal as the Hindu goddess of learning.
satal	A pilgrim's house.
shakti	Shiva's consort. Literally, the dynamic element in the male-female relationship, and the female aspect of the Tantric Absolute.
shikhara	A brick or stone temple of geometrical shape with a tall central spire.
Shitala Mai	A former ogress who became protector of children, worshipped at Swayambhunath.

Shiva	The most awesome of Hindu gods. He destroys all things, good as well as evil, allowing new creation to take shape.
Sita	Rama's wife, heroine of the *Ramayana* epic.
Srawan	The fourth month of the Nepalese year (July - August).
stupa	A bell-shaped relic chamber.
sundhara	A fountain with a golden spout.
Surjya	The sun god, often identified with Vishnu.
suttee	Former practise of immolating widows on their husband's funeral pyres.

T - U

Taleju Bhawani	The Nepalese goddess, originally a South Indian deity; an aspect of Devi.
Tara	Historically a Nepalese princess now deified by Buddhists and Hindus.
Terai	The Nepalese lowland region.
thangka	A religious scroll painting.
tika	A colorful vermilion powder applied by Hindus to the forehead, between the eyes, as a symbol of the presence of the divine.
tole	A street.
topi	The formal, traditional Nepalese cap.
torana	A decorative carved crest suspended over the door of a sanctum, with the figure of the enshrined deity at its center.

V - Z

vajra	In Tantric Buddhism, a ritual thunderbolt or curved sceptre symbolising the Absolute. It also represents power and male energy (also *dorje*).
vihara	A Buddhist monastery, encompassing a *bahal* and a *bahil*.
Vishnu	One of the Hindu trinity, a god who preserves life and world itself. In Nepal, he is most commonly represented as Narayan.
yoni	A hole in a stone symbolizing the female sexual aspect. Usually seen together with a *lingum*.

Index

U, V

W, X, Z

NOTES

NOTES

Kathmandu Valley

4 km/ 2,5 miles